Information Policies
and Strategies

Information Policies and Strategies

Ian Cornelius

facet publishing

© Ian Cornelius 2010

Published by Facet Publishing
7 Ridgmount Street, London WC1E 7AE
www.facetpublishing.co.uk

Facet Publishing is wholly owned by CILIP: the Chartered
Institute of Library and Information Professionals.

British Library Cataloguing in Publication Data
A catalogue record for this book is available
from the British Library.

ISBN 978-1-85604-677-0

First published 2010

Typeset from author's files in 10/15 pt Palermo and Syntax by
Facet Publishing.
Printed and made in Great Britain by MPG Books Group, UK.

For Attracta and Alec

Contents

Preface

THIS IS AN introductory book about information policy. It takes the form of a discussion of the issues that affect the determination of what policy should be, and a discussion of which mechanisms give effect to the intended policy. The aim of the book is to take readers to the point where they can develop the arguments that will lead them to determination of what information policy should be, and where they can develop appropriate policies for the environment they are operating in. This is not a description or explanation of what policies or regulations currently are, or should be, in any jurisdiction. Nor is it a legal or political science or sociological text book, or a review of existing literature. Readers wanting accounts of current law or practice should turn to any of the wide range of excellent studies available. References in the text have been kept to an absolute minimum, and the bibliography is very small. If you want to immerse yourself in reading about any of the issues raised in this book just open a newspaper, or watch the television, where on almost any day you will find matters that involve the generation, transfer, use, storage or retrieval of information and the policy issues that govern them.

This book will be of interest to anyone concerned with information policy. It is relevant to librarians because it deals with issues of censorship and intellectual property. Other readers will find it useful because, although the book does not take the place of dedicated works on any aspect of information policy, it will guide all readers through the process of identifying exactly what they want policy to be and also through the stages of analysis and strategy formation.

The book will also appeal to another type of reader, those whose interest lies in understanding the larger processes at work in an information society. The way information policy interacts with broad conceptualizations of the modern world is discussed to aid campaigners and social theorists. This work is thus also of interest to policy makers and analysts and other parts of the academic community. The easy stance to take, and the default position in this book, is that of the outraged liberal. This is just a rhetorical device to help drive the discussion and to provoke response. Anyone who has to write information policy, as a guide or as a rulebook, will be helped by the analysis here of how we can proceed to identify just what merits policy protection and how we can relate that to the conditions in which we live. The discussion ties realities to intentions and aspirations. The book raises many issues not normally discussed in debates about information policy, and is aimed also at the general reader with an interest in but no previous knowledge of information policy issues.

The book has two main parts, one on macro-level studies of contexts which frame our understanding of what role information policies have in the world we inhabit, and one on micro level studies of sectors and mechanisms that may affect information policies in the real world, as we attempt through legal, cultural, administrative and technological measures to make the high level theories work effectively.

This book owes much to many people. The publishing team at Facet have shown remarkable patience and understanding, as have my family. My students, over many years, have in class discussions given me the insights that have helped me form the approach I take in this book. My colleagues have also contributed much to my understanding of the complex array of issues that make up information policy, and my friends have given me much by their company and good humour. In return, I hope this book adds something to the study of information policy, and that it provides some food for thought for anyone who reads it.

Ian Cornelius

1

Introduction

I N THE SPRING of 2009 a protest in London, England, at the time of an international meeting resulted in the death of a man in the crowd. Later, it emerged that he was not part of the demonstration but had merely been walking home from work. Quite quickly, some video footage appeared showing him being struck and knocked to the ground by a policeman. A few days later another short piece of grainy video appeared, showing a policeman first shoving a woman in the back with his hand and then striking her across the back of her legs with his baton. Quite clearly, this is a story about several different themes. First, it is about concerns over police behaviour; it is also a story about concerns over world economic conditions and the policies of world leaders. But it is also a news story, something that became an information item. As such it has a life, it has to be described and labelled in some way that allows it to be stored and then found again later. That, if you like, is about the management of the item, but we can also ask questions about the nature of the item. What exactly was being videoed? Did the person with the camera focus on just part of a larger scene? There is no sound with the video footage, so we do not know what the woman and the policeman said to one another – we do not have a complete picture, so we lack information about this event.

The policeman wears a coat with no identifying badge or number: it would be impossible to use the footage to isolate which policeman hit the woman, so immediately we want further information to complete our knowledge of the event. Should we get that? Is this selective footage the kind of thing that, contrary to the general interests of public order, dents confidence in the police, so much that we might want to suppress such video clips? The woman is identifiable, so putting the video clip on a social network website (YouTube) is in some way an invasion of her privacy; she could find herself on police files for her activities that day, and maybe other shadowy groups would also want to identify her for some other purpose. Someone took the footage and could be said to own it. What rights do they have over any and every use of the clip on news TV programmes and in newspapers? Could it be said that this is an event of general public interest, in many different ways, and that society at large should 'own' the clip, it should pass into the general public domain? This was just one of several stories that surfaced in the news at that time concerning information policy. On another occasion a doctor attempting to enter the UK to run workshops on euthanasia (he was intending to speak in Bournemouth, a coastal town for retired folk with potentially a good client base for such business) was stopped at the airport and refused admission. Euthanasia, and assisting someone to commit suicide, are criminal offences in the UK. The doctor claimed this was a denial of the right of free expression (he was eventually allowed to enter). Do we want to allow people to speak on matters that are illegal? It is common that people are barred from countries if they incite hatred or advocate violence against any group or country, so where do we draw the line?

Almost at the same time, in the broadsheet press, concern was raised about the activities of Google in its agreement with major libraries and publishers to allow it to create digital versions of almost all the world's books (or those in English, at least). This monopoly on digital access constituted a potentially dangerous trend for scholars whose ideological position has always been to allow open access to knowledge – as long as appropriate acknowledgements are made and royalties paid. At almost any time a similar range of stories, often news events apparently on completely different subjects, could be found that contain some element that relates to the governance of information. We pass them by every day, yet if we were to stop and think it would be clear that these are important issues, they affect, and in some cases heavily influence or control, our lives, and we want to know what is going on. Yet, they are complex: it takes time to consider all the issues connected with intellectual property rights and all the other issues that have been mentioned here. If we are to make our voice heard in determining how we regulate these matters we need to be able to formulate sensible and sustainable statements about them. That is why we all need to know about information policy. We need to know how to analyse the situations in which information policy issues are likely to arise; we need to know how to understand the effects that policies we pursue as societies might have; and we need to know how to determine what those policies ought to be. We also need to know how to determine what strategies to follow to bring those policies about.

Information policy is a dry and abstract term; it seems remote from everyday concerns and probably outside our control. Occasionally special issues – like censorship of the internet, or data protection – rise up to claim some part of the centre stage, but no information issue dominates or directs government policy for long. But actually we experience information policy daily, and it affects our life styles, our political choices, our shopping, as well as other issues that we negotiate or navigate our way through, like health or education. Other terms cloud the picture because they are closely related and seem to overlap. You might have a policy of always reading a bedtime story to your children, or putting all your music on your laptop computer, or filing all your household bills for one year, or shredding all statements with identifiable financial information. All these might be policies, but they might be strategies, or they might be information management practices, or they might be a combination of policies, strategies and information management practices, depending on which way you look at the issue. We all, instinctively as well as deliberately, do things which come under the label of information policy: in this book we will examine what those issues are and the ways we can look at them. We will do so with the intention of working out how to make sensible decisions and statements about the way we govern the use of information – in short, we will work out how to write information policies. We will be raising our consciousness about information issues in general and finding tools that help explain how information issues can be perceived. We will also work out how to formulate our own information policies and strategies. As a start let us say that information policy includes all ways that affect the generation, dissemination and use of information.

How governments control information policies

Most obviously it is government regulations and the laws passed by legislatures that affect how information can be accessed. Here we are using the term 'government' as a shorthand to refer to all the mechanisms of the state – including legislatures, executive authorities both central and local, state-owned or state-controlled institutions, and the mechanisms for enforcing the law. We will discriminate between these later; for the moment we will just use the shorthand. That government influence is felt in several ways.

We can identify four main government influences on information policies:

- Governments are the greatest single producers of information in most countries.
- Governments are also the greatest consumers of information.
- Governments have access to the greatest collective stores of information – about us individually and about us collectively.
- Governments control matters like education and communications and, to a lesser extent, technology.

There are information issues that governments do not control, or do not have sufficient control over, or where they have failed to garner enough information.

First, governments produce more information than anyone else in any jurisdiction. That information includes documents, regulations, laws, treaties, records of legislative proceedings, reports of government-sponsored enquiries, advice leaflets on citizen entitlements, advice on what to do in emergencies, school curricula, records of what various agencies have done, accounts, plans and so on. The list is so extensive that there is almost nothing in your daily life that is not affected one way or another by government activity. Even if you shred or burn every official document that comes through the mail to you, you will still be using government-produced information when you go down the road and observe lane markings or street signs. If your country has no government-owned media the media that do exist will be regu-lated by some government-sponsored agency that shares out the wave-bands and checks content.

Second, governments consume information and they alone have the coercive power to garner information; in particular they consume infor-mation about us, partly because they need it to raise taxes or armies or plan school capacities, but also because we ask them to do things in our interest, like protect us from data theft, give us welfare benefits, and license us to drive motor vehicles. The character of the current age is to require us to surrender information about ourselves in order to participate in standard forms of social intercourse, whether it be opening a bank account, getting married or using a telephone. The trail of data can form an identity that puts us at risk if that identity is compromised by expo-sure or corruption of the data. Governments have most of our documented identity but we need them to act to secure that data.

This is a critical component of the things we have to discuss. Our need for protection over data, and the risks that are posed by the existence of 'data identities', show that we need to intervene in the information policy process at national and international level, as well as to be involved in the formation of policies for our immediate daily life and work concerns. This raises another question: if we have documented identities, then that takes the form of a number of independent items of information, some of which are created in the process of use. For example, mobile phone records show where you have been as well as who you sent or received calls or messages from, and the record of your use is documentary evidence that is created not only every time you use the device but also every time the phone automatically registers with a new signalling station as you move around. Our identity – in this case what our characteristic movements are – consists of a number of simple pieces of information, some not created intentionally or knowingly by us – that make our identity when they are gathered together. So, we must consider as a matter of concern for regulation the question of who has the power to gather that information together, and whether there are incomplete and misleading 'documented' identities being created. One example is the submission of information to government agencies. There is a principle that information submitted for one purpose may not be used for another, so the information you pass to the driving licence agency may not be passed to the health bureau. Yet, we might think it a good thing if the driving licence agency had a record of the health condition of every potential driver, so that in emergencies appropriate medical aid can be provided, and also for the protection of other road users so that licences are not issued to those whose medical condition might make them a danger to other road users. This shows another problem with information: the questions about information use are often not just information questions. You might ask if information policy is concerned with only those matters that are strictly information matters, yet it may be difficult to disentangle the other issues from general information questions. We see that deciding questions about information policy becomes more complex. A final point is the question of format. Does information have to be in tangible form for it to be subject to information policy? A quick review shows that this is not possible.

Questions about which books to stock in the local library, what documents to protect from inappropriate access, even which records of activity – like phone use – to keep safe may seem simple. Yet, we cannot say that if a book is banned then broadcasts of readings from the book are not, just because they are in a different format. The question is again more complex, because what is publicly acceptable in one medium may not be considered suitable in another. A book may inspire a film that becomes much more lurid than the original book, and the film may be banned or restricted even when the book is not – and the film script may be treated differently from either. In this little discussion we have raised another matter that will become quite central to many questions of information policy formation – public taste and moral judgement. It seems that the principles for the formation of information policy will be influenced by taste, the need to maintain public order, and moral judgements relating to non-information issues.

A third way in which governments affect the flow of information is that they have a collective picture of everyone: they control masses of data and can see an overall picture not visible to others. This gives them the power to act, which we cannot challenge unless we have access to the same information. Making information available therefore becomes an important part of the way we think our countries should be run: we believe in democratic participation and the responsibility of citizens to contribute to the resolution of national or public issues – most obviously when we vote.

There are two other ways in which government affects the flow of information: first, in its control of – or at least financial power over – other policies, such as education policy and communications policies; second, rather perversely, in the way it does not have access to or control over information, for example when it does not have control over what is made public on the internet, or because it does not have data critical for public policy, like the rate of illegal immigration. So, we should consider government generation, use and control of certain types of *data*, and we need also to know about control and regulation of *content* – whether it is school textbooks, TV programmes, internet sites or your private photographic collection.

Finally, there is also a question of form: if the streets are littered with pizza adverts, double-glazing adverts or election manifestos, is that an information policy question or a public order question?

Other bodies that generate and control information

Governments regulate and legislatures pass laws, but there are other bodies generating information and controlling information about us that we need to consider. Some of these are very large and are in themselves public policy issues – like Google, Microsoft, telecommunication companies, internet service providers, large media corporations or banks, or any agency that has a potentially controlling position in the general process of creating, disseminating and using information. Others are smaller players who, usually contracted to a larger organization, can lose, delay, disclose, hamper access to or hide information we need access to or need to have secured. In this complex picture we obviously need the right mix of mechanisms that ensure the right access and protection. But what is that? There must be principles that govern what effect we want to produce, and there are probably bigger movements, maybe large-scale multi-generational explanations of the movement of events that give us a framework to understand what is happening, what is possible and what is desirable. Within this global picture we work and live our lives, attempting to understand, explain, get right and implement what we think are the best ways to handle information we have or need. And, of course, we may be many actors in this complex picture; at home we want to relax and watch or read, at work we may have to determine the use of data and access to it, and we may in some other corporate capacity influence discussion about regulation. These differing roles may actually be in conflict. In this book we shall pick our way through the complexity to a position where we can formulate statements of policy or strategy about information.

Information policy as about any means by which the generation, distribution, and use of information is regulated

We need to narrow down to some concrete areas that very broad description that states information policy to be about any means by which the generation, distribution and use of information is regulated. There are some staple components or sectors, and the way we perceive them and their significance depends in part on how you approach the question of information policy. The staple areas, those that attract most public attention, are censorship and freedom of expression, data protection and privacy, intellectual property rights and freedom of information. These areas are legislated for nationally and are the subjects of international agreements; they may also be subject to local norms and customs and special exceptions or arrangements that arise through convenience or historical accident. For example, although there are standard arrangements in the UK for copyright of printed materials with an agreed European standard expiry date for the payment of royalties, there is a perpetual copyright in *Peter Pan*, whereby the royalties go towards the funding of the Great Ormond Street Children's Hospital in London. This seems like a good cause and so the exception is tolerated.

There are other areas concerned less with content or protection of information and more with control of finite resources, such as broadcasting policy, or with regulating the carriage of information, such as telecommunications policy. In the first group we are concerned directly with the content, its protection or disclosure; in the second group (and there are others we can add to it) our concern is primarily with the regulation of transmission, even though there may be concerns about content (for example, it is internationally agreed that certain potentially harmful goods may not be transmitted through the mail). If you decide that it is important that you read to your children, or with them, at bedtime, rather than letting them listen to a tape, disc or other medium, you are concerned about transmission, although you may have other objectives about inculcating good reading habits or bonding with the children, or just checking that they are in good shape at the end of the day.

A final group of sectors of interest to information policy is more remote from immediate concerns about content, even though content and transmission are critical for these sectors. For example, governments regulate education policy, something that is obviously very much bound up with information, especially when standards and curricula are being set. Is this part of information policy? You might rightly be concerned if your child is being taught out-of-date science at school because older and outdated books are being used, but that seems to be a different sort of question from ones about censorship or the right to enjoy the income from use of intellectual property. Similarly, governments usually have some sort of policy about technology, particularly computers and other information-handling technologies. These policy issues too seem not to be in the same class of questions as those in the first group we listed. Finally, governments, legislatures or constitutions sometimes regulate religious policy, either through the management of a state church or through the need to regulate competing religious claims, practices that might interfere with other aspects of life, or the use of religious schools. This itself raises a completely different set of questions.

What non-governmental agencies do within the realm of information policy

We can turn away from governments to consider what non-governmental agencies do that might come within the realm of information policy. Shops, companies, large corporations, charities, clubs and associations all advertise, either themselves (a brand) or their products. Sometimes they have intellectual property in their names – Rolls-Royce cars have a logo that is worth protecting, as do major brands across the commercial spectrum, and some groups have property in a name (Champagne, for example). Many organizations handle data about individuals that needs care in control in use just as much as anything we surrender to the government. Financial information is obviously very important. We need, as a society and in the interests of individuals, to regulate these activities. For example, we need to control false advertising.

This introduces another point that needs examination: we treat different kinds of information in different ways – for example, we allow politicians at election time to make any kind of statement, including the obviously inaccurate, whereas we would never allow advertisers the same freedom. That suggests that we treat information in different ways, according to context. In turn, this also raises a question about who information policy is for. We could argue that information policies, as part of general government policy, should operate to make government more efficient, in the interests of the taxpayer and the country. Alternatively we could argue that information policies should operate in the interests of commerce, to maximize the wealth-generating capacity of the country. As we are commonly held to be in an information age in which information helps generate wealth this might seem natural.

Thirdly, there might be an argument that although both these claims are good they might at times conflict, and thus there has to be some middle way that serves the common good rather than a particular interest. Actually, a fourth approach is the most immediately fruitful, because it takes us into the subject from our own viewpoint, that of the citizen and consumer. In this approach we seek to make information policies serve and protect the interests of individuals, whereby we ascribe information rights to everyone. Many of these rights are identified as intrinsic components of human, civic and social rights in general in international treaties and conventions. Although this seems straightforward we must also remember that as citizens we are also members of other groups and may still find a conflict in the interplay of our rights according to the role we play.

Information policy must provide for different sorts of needs

As a citizen and consumer you need the protection and opportunities that proper regulation of all information activities, public and private, will provide. As an employee or entrepreneur you may need a quite different climate, and the two may be in conflict. Information policy must provide for all needs, but we commonly find that the different approaches are also nuanced by the traditions in any one jurisdiction – whereas one country might have a tradition of openness, which might be sharply amended by certain experiences such as war, or those of 11 September 2001 in the USA, another country may have a tradition of strong protection of persons from information thought to be harmful, and a third may be careless of information issues, regarding them as insignificant.

At this stage we can ask what the literature shows us about attitudes to the formation of information policy, but before that we can expand on the definition of some of the staple areas mentioned above to show what issues come to the fore when we try to regulate them. The complexities that emerge as we investigate these areas throw up a number of other questions through which we must also navigate our way if we are to find a reasonable and successful way of analysing them and constructing statements and policies about them. As we explore these areas a little more – and there will be deeper investigation later in the book – we encounter bizarre variations in what constitutes information. This is no place to go into discussions about the concept of information or its definition in any prescriptive sense. Here we need to convey a sense of the range of things that can count as information, and we can start with a common notion that we want to regulate those things that have a tangible form as documents. Unfortunately that soon disintegrates as an umbrella use because of variations in media, format and the context of use.

Information policy, public policy and other disciplines

Two final points to consider are the questions of whether information policy is a part of general public policy, and whether it can be reduced to the subject approaches of other disciplines such as law, politics or sociology. The answer to the first question must be that, although it is in part a public policy issue, that picture is obscured by three factors. First, many information policy issues are part of something else, which may be public policy in its own right but which is quite different from information policy. This may be because, the second point to raise here, the information policy questions are to be seen in a very different time frame from other aspects of public policy, which normally relate to short or medium term issues that rarely extend beyond ten to 15 years. Third, there is very rarely any attempt to establish a general information policy, even as an overall plan or strategy. Information issues are usually legislated separately, and in a pluralist democracy we may be happier to have it that way. Sometimes there are attempts, as in the UK with the Copyright, Designs and Patents Act of 1988, to bring a number of related issues together, but it would be extraordinary to find legislation or even a general government plan that covered intellectual property, censorship, data protection, freedom of information, broadcasting and all the other issues that we could corral within the general umbrella term information policy. That raises some other questions. If information policy is not part of public policy, what is it? Is it just a general frame of enquiry? Or is it an artificial creation, something that never did have a separate identifiable existence? Most likely, it is because we have an interest in the way we govern the creation, distribution and use of information, and we want to consider all these things together. A different term, like information governance, may seem more appropriate, except that it has never caught on and has no currency, but we don't actually govern information, it seems to have some life of its own; we really do have a policy towards it, and some things we can control through legislation, others we can only form general frameworks for. We can have a general policy for transport, and bring together canals, roads, flights, trains, buses, cycle paths, motor traffic management and so on, but we can't control information in the same way – we don't know what new content will emerge, or how it will be used and how that will affect us. The content is not so easily manageable, and new forms of use are always emerging. For example, in a time when data protection is more important than ever, and when more of us have a concern about how data about us is being used or is at risk, we find, with the use of social networking software like Facebook, Twitter, Bebo, MySpace, Flickr, YouTube and so on, that more of us are making public more information about ourselves than ever before, and in a way that is easily taken for use for identity theft. This changed use is quite outside any regulatory framework. All we can do is take into account new use patterns as we consider how we are to protect personal data. We see here the impact not only of new technology, as phenomena like the universal growth and adoption of mobile (cellular or portable) phone ownership and use, but also the applications of new technology, as with the range of user-friendly applications broadly known as Web 2.0. We don't know what may come next; legislation is always one step behind technological advance, and the dysfunctional use of new opportunities that we call crime also always seems a step ahead of any regulation.

The second question, whether information policy can be reduced to other disciplines, is more complex. Obviously, we consider and use the techniques of law, politics, ethics, many aspects of the study of society and social studies of technology, and also aspects of economics when we look at trade in data. Information policy does not have a methodology of its own; it is really just a problem to study, complicated by our own split attitude towards the issues that are raised. Rarely does an information policy issue emerge that is merely for discussion, the object of curiosity: usually we have an attitude, a concern, and we are seeking to change practices, to make things better. Thus, we have a campaigning approach to these questions. Somehow we must accept that we have both an object of dispassionate enquiry, as we seek to understand what is happening and perhaps to offer some explanation of it, and there is also the likelihood of a campaigning aspect to what we do.

Two points to make in relation to any other disciplines are, first, that none of them have as their objective the explication of information policy, or even of component issues, and second that none of them can encompass the range of issues we wish to consider when reviewing information policy. A study of law, or politics, will not reveal how to construct information policy. So, it seems best to put information policy within the information sciences and to treat it as an interdisciplinary and applied area of study. The record of investigation into information policies suggests that the lack of any firm disciplinary or interdisciplinary base does tweak the character of enquiry. In the University of Wisconsin-Milwaukee, for example, the Centre for Information Policy Research is very closely related to the discussion of ethical issues and questions. Resting information policy analysis on the firm foundations of other fields can help but may also hinder what we do. Information policy would not be alone in making extensive use of other fields of investigation. Law, for example, obviously something of great concern to the information policy community, makes extensive use of philosophy, psychology, politics, criminology and other disciplines, but eventually makes decisions based on what the 'thick' tradition of law suggests is right: law does not surrender itself to other intellectual traditions, even when making use of them. We can follow that example. Sometimes the questions that emerge, although obviously information questions, may also seem to be more strongly another sort of question. The question of whether we should allow people to view certain images that show children being physically or sexually abused is an information question – people are accessing records, and we take the view that they should not be able to access them. But generally we regard that not as primarily an information question but one of morality and criminality, closely connected to the protection of children. Similarly, the question of whether sex and violence on television adversely affect the behaviour of viewers, particularly children, has been endlessly investigated and debated, but more so by moralists, psychologists and sociologists than information people. A generation ago a British librarian, Douglas Foskett, had a phrase for the library profession to indicate its stance towards the content of records – 'No morals, no politics, no religion' – suggesting that librarians were not for communism, or against apartheid, or in favour of the dissemination of nuclear technology, or opposed to any religion. Their stance was that they just coped with the management of access to the records: the questions about the existence of those records were left to others. Of course, in private librarians might have had strong feelings about some of those issues, but the pretence was that such attitudes had no place in professional practice. Actually, librarians do have an implicit ideological stance towards records and information: they are in favour of them, and they broadly believe that people should have open access to knowledge and information. In this respect they have a campaigning attitude towards information, coloured by attitudes towards its proper management (securing private data, disclosing public information) that requires them, like any other member of society, to have a way of understanding how we should handle these information questions, and what information policies we should formulate and implement. So, we can say that information questions do not collapse into any other field of enquiry, but they are broad issues that relate to the construction of civil society: we all have an interest in how information policy works.

Conclusion

We began by talking about issues of policy, strategy and management in relation to information, and it is time to start separating these so we know exactly what we are focusing on. As noted above, you can make a decision to collect a certain type of record or material, in a certain format, and that could be either a policy or a strategy, or an information management decision. The information management decision is really concentrated on the material in hand and does not concern any reaction to the content. So, if you create a document by making some marks on a paper, you can then describe the marks, make comments about their generation, storage and subject relationship, and annotate the whole record with a comment about how to store it, how it came into your possession, and any other comment about the contents, for example that it is secret, part of a series or a suppressed document, either because the author chose not to disclose it or because it was officially banned. But in the act of managing information you are unlikely to make any decision as to whether the document should be banned; that is made in a different context, the context of policy and strategy. These last two terms can lead to confusion, and it is not clear how we can set them in an easily secured relation. In connection with other issues we may decide, because we have another question in mind, to follow a certain strategy in relation to some information issue – yet if we were to consider that information issue alone, we might determine the same line of action to be a policy.

Consider the question of dividing up the broadcast spectrum. We might have a view that such a sensitive matter is best kept wholly in the hands of agencies accountable to the democratically elected government, and that the media, if not actually operated by the state, should at least be operated in the public interest, and should follow a policy of what was generally felt to be in the public interest, as determined by public debate. That would be a policy; the operating activities of the broadcaster that were intended to achieve this might be a strategy. But in another approach one might say that it is against the interests of the people that governments control the media, that there should be as many independent broadcasting operations as possible, that none of them should be controlled by the state, and that the public interest was best ensured by whatever secured the independent operations of these stations. Yet how do you decide who gets access to such a finite resource as the broadcast spectrum? There has to be a higher policy decision.

Another question relates to the operating context. Even if we agree to have independent stations we may feel that we want to control the mix of what is broadcast, so instead of allowing a station to broadcast (let us be ridiculous here) a single repetitive message, all day every day, we might want to insist that as the broadcast spectrum is 'ours' we dictate that there be a mixture of programmes – not all music, not all one type of music, some discussion programmes, some news, and some local general interest information about traffic or jobs, or education. These are decisions about information content but they are not decisions made in the name of information, they are made in relation to general social need – the interest of society – and they will relate to the general context of information exchange. The media will feed off what material is available and make selection decisions based on what their operating policy is. Just as the local public library or local newspaper decides to buy this and not that book, or to go with this local and not that remote story, so they feed from the general world of information exchange. How do we determine what of that will be available? More interestingly, how do we understand the general world context in which all this information exchange takes place? Looking at that question is the task of the next chapters.

Part 1

Contexts for information policy

RARELY DOES ANY information issue arise that is divorced from any connection with other questions. Even with seemingly clear information issues like censorship, the control of content, the context is critical. How critical will become apparent when we consider international information rights.

Understanding the international contexts

Understanding the contexts is important if we are to comprehend the total information picture, and important if we are to analyse what information policies and strategies should be. Let us start with two simple statements. First, information issues are about utterances, but they are also about ideas. Second, the current information context is strongly influenced by international trade and the internationalization of technology through global provision of access to communication media. We need ways of understanding these and there are three that we will discuss in Part 1:

- the idea of an information society and its impact on the regulation of information

■ the idea of a public sphere in which ideas are communicated and
  messages exchanged
■ the idea of information rights.

Let us consider first the association between utterances and ideas. We cannot separate any statement from the medium it appears in, and we cannot isolate a statement in any medium or format from all other forms of
that statement, or the context in which it acquires meaning. In the previous chapter the instance of separating the book from the film or the
web page was mentioned, but we must go further and identify the social
attitude towards some texts – sacred texts or legal testimony, for example – and the process by which a document can appear before you. The
newspaper in your hand is a by-product of a long sequence of actions
by which journalists observe events, write up or compose copy, perhaps
including not only a description of the event but also some commentary
and analysis, and send that copy electronically to the newspaper office
where decisions about the content of the next issue and each individual
page are made. Then pages are laid out, there may be decisions to excise
some content and include local specific content for regional issues, and
the electronic tape is distributed to printing outlets where the paper is
finally produced, distributed and sold. As you look at the paper you
understand the format ('this is a newspaper'); you understand the particular paper and its editorial style and political persuasion; and because
it is a newspaper you understand that this is one in a long sequence of
issues of this paper. The way you regard the paper in your hand is set
by recognizing the association of that particular set of impressions on paper
with all the circumstances of its intellectual and physical production,
but also with its relationship to the total world of news reporting, print
publications and communication within societies. It is, effectively, the idea
of the newspaper that commands your approach to it.

Newspapers thrive by publishing information not available elsewhere, particularly about government actions. The revelation of information not previously disclosed by governments, or indeed other groups

that command our attention because they are important for us, is akin to the disclosure of a secret, something that should not be disclosed. Typically, a game is played whereby news media disclose that which might embarrass governments or members of them, but the media do not disclose what they regard as important national secrets – the negotiating strategy to be followed at an upcoming international meeting or treaty negotiation, the tactical plans of police or military, or private data of ordinary citizens. What is it that enables us to identify something not previously known to us as a secret that should not be disclosed? What enables us to agree that a news report reveals enough but not too much of state activity? We understand the game that is being played, and the implicit rules of that game. We engage in a form of life where the frontiers of what it is permissible to say are understood, and the importance of playing up to that line is emphasized. We expect thorough and critical exposure and examination of what governments do, within bounds of loyalty and betrayal, boundaries that we implicitly know. In 18th-century Britain it was illegal to publish the proceedings of parliament, to disclose the business or who said what. Now we would feel it an assault on our idea of democracy if we did not have full and constant access to parliamentary proceedings. The frontiers have changed but the rules of the game remain similar.

This situation is nuanced not only by time but also by location: the tacit rules of what may be said in London are different even from those that determine what may be said in the USA, or in Ireland. These tacit rules sometimes have formal expression in laws, regulations, treaties and other legal decisions, but they are also governed by custom. A British observer of American election behaviour would be astonished at the permitted level of what in Britain would be called personal abuse and intrusion into the private life of candidates. The differences that emerge between societies with far greater variations – say in language and historical experience – are obviously greater, even though a wide range of variations might be understood within a loose grouping like the phrase 'western democracies'. What can be said, and how it can be said, is an important feature of the variation between different information regimes. That process is brought into sharp relief by the proximity we now experience to all other forms of social life on the planet as technology and international movement in people, goods and ideas bring us, apparently, closer together, or at least erode some aspects of the impact of distance.

Globalization and technology

The record of technological innovation in information products and the growth in information services over the last 20 years needs no reiteration. The impact of globalization has been attested and is in our own daily experience as we send e-mail messages around the globe, or buy cheap clothing of Asian manufacture or watch TV news footage of disasters, wars and even New Year celebrations from distant places. Figures produced now will probably be out of date before they reach print, and the point here is not to prove the existence of this globalization phenomenon but to comment on its implications for information policy. No one needs reminders of the global effect of economic developments, or the international speed of transmission of viruses, including computer viruses, although it is said that bad financial news spreads quicker than anything else – another information phenomenon.

Up to a generation ago there was some element of protectionism over information products and services that resulted in some developing nations imposing frontier controls over western goods and services. Everyone had had enough experience of the importation of Hollywood movies to know that this particular form of cultural imperialism was worth guarding against. Some countries, such as Brazil, attempted to impose severe restrictions on the importation of software and computer hardware in an effort to stimulate local industry. In the change that came about everyone wanted to be in the loop; no one wanted to be outside the international flow of information.

True, there had to be some international agreements about the use of space for satellites and controls over illegal and harmful content, but these regulatory efforts proceeded quickly enough to secure an international market in information goods and services, even though serious issues remain, both at the national level (the French do not like the importation of cheap American TV programmes as they undercut and threaten their own film and TV programming industry) and at international level (the question of tariffs for mobile phones and the seemingly intractable problem of internet content and clogging of traffic with high volumes of pornography, spam and banal content). Luckily, or unluckily, the exponential leaps in technological capacity to store and transmit, and the apparent improvement in search engines, have allowed us to avoid confrontation with these problems except when they become excessively vexatious. But we will have to confront these problems and we will have to know what to do. A first step to that is to understand the character of the age we are in and to offer some explanatory frameworks for comprehending the current fetish over information. Some knowledge of arguments about the information society and knowledge economies becomes essential.

2

Globalization and information societies

WHEN WE SPEAK of globalization we should understand exactly how the term is being employed, as this will affect our understanding of how information policies should be shaped, understood or changed. A similar caution applies to our use of the terms public sphere and information society.

Globalization can be used to describe a recent phenomenon that has transformed much of international life, or at least has transformed much discussion about the impact globally of changes in the world economy and especially in financial services. If the term really is used to describe these transformations it should be a shorthand for a very complex set of changes, and it might be more common to speak of subsets of the overall phenomenon that relate to particular sectors. We are immediately in territory where extreme care is advised. Such descriptions, and we would want to know that they are accurate and comprehensive, may indeed describe current changes or conditions, but the image so created will predispose us to select certain policy options in a very wide range of sectors. Any description will seek the authority of accuracy and comprehensiveness but may also seek the persuasiveness of being predictive as well as explanatory: our simple term 'globalization' suddenly becomes something close to a model and goes well beyond being a mere description.

A second temptation, beyond accepting a plausible model of recent world changes, is to accept that the term, in this case 'globalization', but it might also be 'information society', goes well beyond being a mere model to explain current changes and predict future movements. It is actually a concept that embraces far more than changes in volume or direction and in fact amounts to a substantive qualitative change in our society across the globe. When 'globalization' is used like this we are being asked to accept that models, understandings, explanations and expectations are to be jettisoned in favour of a new understanding not only of the situation as it is, but also of how the interplay of economic, cultural, social, political and financial forces will work in future and what substantial differences we must accept as the basis for our own future actions and decision making in consequence. This interplay can work in two ways. First, there is the simple assertion, for example, that a result of the recent world economic crisis will be the significant transfer of economic power and initiative from the West to the East. Second, there is a more complex set of claims that assert these changes to have been in progress over a longer period of time and that they will lead to a more sophisticated set of changes and responses from the various participants, including the possibility that, for example, western countries may develop more elaborate responses to the apparent change in economic circumstances that will maintain their political and economic dominance. Current campaigns to require China and India to adhere to carbon emission restrictions would be an example. How can that be an information policy issue? It is so because it involves controls over the transfer of knowledge, which is ultimately an information policy issue.

Let us turn from these caveats, which must be kept in hand in general matters but which also apply directly to issues of globalization, to consider first ideas about the information society and then ideas about the public sphere. Currently debate includes discussion of the idea that concepts of globalization supersede any claims that the interpretation of the current age is best understood as an information society or public sphere issue.

Information societies and information policy

We do not need to rehearse the catalogue of events and figures for production or traffic that indicate we are in an information age. We can give a moment to pause over the question of whether this is the only information age, and we can readily consider the developments in telephones, telegraphy, print production and film in the 19th century to be a serious rival to claims that our current age is the only age. What we can say is that it is only in the last 50 years that we have had explanations of economic or societal development that put information centre stage. In giving us these arguments their proponents have made discussion of information immensely more complicated.

The idea of an information society

The idea of an information society is usually held to originate with the work carried out by Fritz Machlup (1962). The debate rapidly moved on from those early studies of US economic output in the late 1950s, both by broadening the academic base away from purely economic analysis to include sociological and related studies, and also by extending the period under discussion to include earlier as well as later periods. In the late 1970s a very comprehensive study attempted to understand the whole range of US economic and productive activity as an information or non-information concern. Debate also became more sophisticated as it attempted to become more predictive as well as explanatory, and as it included attempts to explain social changes in information terms – see in particular Nico Stehr's *Knowledge Societies* (1995). That title itself hints at other ways of naming the phenomena under discussion, and the current favourite, 'knowledge economies', seen by some as a way out of the current economic hiccup in advanced economies, follows on from 'post-industrial societies', 'information age' and other similar word combinations. A generation of publishing activity has produced a large literature that includes predictive as well as explanatory works, and claims that range from serious well grounded academic studies to simple sensationalist futurology. Many of these works have disappeared into the remote storage of large libraries, but others, like the work of Machlup, command our attention, both at the level of research and also as popularising and mediating studies.

Some authors, rejecting the notion that the various names for the phenomenon were all synonyms, attempted to use some subset of these terms to describe different stages of unfolding developments in late 20th-century capitalist societies. We should not forget either that Marxist analysis also had an interpretation of the phenomena which had changes in the significance of the use of knowledge or information as the central element in explanations of what in Marxist terms would be late capitalist society. For our purposes we need not get too immersed in the details of these debates but we should note their two central features – first, the importance of the transfer of knowledge, and second, the dominant role of knowledge generation and distribution in economic development.

The picture becomes quite complex and serves as a reminder of the importance of information policies. We learn, for example, that even traditional industries like agriculture became highly dependent on not only the generation of new knowledge by science but also the development of new knowledge-based products, like pesticides, fungicides, herbicides, insecticides and fertilizers, and also on a mechanism to disseminate this knowledge to the working farmer, either by advertising, formal professional education, advisory services, consultancy services or subcontracting arrangements. The knowledge contained in the product is itself of little use without the ancillary knowledge of how and when to apply it, so the realm of expertise is extended and the idea of what has to be packaged with any new knowledge extends our notion of what has to be distributed for the new science in agriculture to work. There is also a darker side to this that must consider the social consequences of the misuse of such information – the use of fertilizer as explosives is a simple example, the development and misuse of biological weapons a highly dangerous example, and the political and military consequences of fears about such weapons have had a marked impact on the world in the last ten years.

Are we, in consequence, to ban the development of such knowledge, or restrict access to it for fear of the spread of such weapons? There have been extensive efforts, which continue to be made, to halt the spread of nuclear weapons technology. The grounds advanced for such a ban relate as much to the political stability of individual regimes, and the potential instability in the world, as to the inherent knowledge itself. Developing information policy becomes obviously important, and the central importance of the development of advanced knowledge within the information society fuels discussion that developing nations might want to access this knowledge and associated technologies.

This brings us back to discussion of the basic ideas about an information society. We can talk of two separate strands: claims made about the idea of an information society, and claims made about the characteristics of such a society. In the first case we should note in particular the claim that new and enhanced levels of wealth creation are associated directly, and almost exclusively, with the development of the information side of any economy or society. The second part of this first set of claims is that in a dialectic of development from agricultural through industrial to information society it is possible to leapfrog the second stage, so closely associated with the dominant nations of the 19th and 20th centuries, and to advance from a mainly agricultural economy directly to an information economy, and the enhanced wealth creation it brings, without the intervening extensive and expensive period of industrial development. Such a leapfrog development would save much social upheaval and potential political and social instability as well as the direct expense and delay of going through an industrial phase. An added attraction is the claim that movement of a traditional agrarian society, and the institutional forms of governance it would have, directly to an information society would also bring with it direct movement to a stage of advanced democracy akin to the level of political development common in advanced western industrial societies.

A further aspect of these claims needs to be spelled out here: that the claim about an information society, at least in some of its manifestations, is itself a knowledge-based claim. The knowledge being deployed here is that analysis of economic activity first used by Clark in the 1940s to show that the primary source of employment in the USA moved from being agricultural to industrial sometime in the early 20th century, and that the dominance of the industrial sector of the workforce ended in the 1940s with the rise of service industries (Clark, 1940). Daniel Bell (1973) took this basic analysis and added the role of the information sector, which includes both services such as education and medicine but also equipment production, such as computers and medical technology. Bell was able to produce a graph that showed the information sector becoming dominant in the 1960s. We should note, as an aside, that the dominant sector in this model is greater than any of the other sectors but does not include an absolute majority of the workforce. The dialectic that represents development of advanced societies as going through several stages, culminating in the information stage, is redolent of the Marxist dialectic about the development of societies and, at least on the evidence analysed by Bell, seems more plausibly true. The apparent possibility that the stages of the dialectic could be conflated or even excised appealed to analysts of developing societies and could be a potent political weapon.

Characteristics of an information society

We should now return to consider claims about the characteristics of an information society. One has already been mentioned, the distribution of the workforce. We have also mentioned the central claim that new wealth is now created through the application of knowledge or information rather than, as had previously been understood, through the application of financial capital. At a simple level this claim is easily understood: if the knowledge of materials and their properties is improved, and the knowledge about the capacity to manufacture new materials is extended, then it might be possible, say, to use the same amount of material as was previously needed to make one bridge to make two bridges. You would thus have halved the cost of bridge construction, or you could build twice as many bridges with the same investment. It might even be more extensive a saving if the time taken to construct the bridge was similarly cut. Typically the investment in new knowledge yields a more complex picture of returns in more extensive aspects of social life. The effect is what Daniel Bell calls the central principle in the economic sector of western societies, the desire to economize, to get more for less.

As it happens, although many impressive bridges have been built since Bell first published his key study, *The Coming of Post-Industrial Society*, in 1973, the most marked scientific developments since then have been in two different areas: micro (and now nano) technologies, particularly in micro processor technologies and ICT (information and communication technologies) generally, and in bio-molecular sciences, particularly in pharmaceutical applications. There have been other developments in aspects of the social sciences, particularly in financial management, affecting governments, world trade (associated with the idea of globalization) and the financial management of knowledge production itself. This area of development, in financial management, has gone spectacularly wrong in the last 18 months, casting doubt and gloom over any claim that knowledge of financial management has advanced, but the economies where most new knowledge is produced, where most economic advances have been made and where employment in knowledge-based industries has expanded most markedly are those with the largest financial industries. This, effectively, makes policy about the distribution of financial information of particular importance.

A second claim about employment is that the character of employment changes. Bell noted the rise in the sheer numbers, twice the rate of increase in employment in general in the USA in the 1950s and 1960s, among engineers and technologists. More recently the government of Ireland has called for a doubling of the numbers of PhDs by 2013, as part of the drive to adapt the Irish economy to the so-called 'smart economy' (the latest phrase in the long history of terms to describe the phenomenon of information). The continued importance of a scientifically skilled work-force has implications for education policy, which must deploy to students at all stages of formal education the latest scientific knowledge.

Information policy then needs to consider moving from a permissive format, merely allowing information to be exchanged, to one where there is an imperative to make effective rapid transfer of the best information to those who need it most. This might be through traditional means such as formal education but could also be through new technologies such as personal information media and personalized Web 2.0 applications like social networking sites. A vast amount of knowledge and information on what might be called DIY issues, such as gardening, cooking, home improvements, personal skill enhancements like learning a foreign language, and cultural information, has always been made available through libraries and also through television services; information might now be made available in ways other than through permissive intervention. Is it an information policy issue – a question about which we need to take a well-reasoned position – to be more than permissive in allowing information access? Traditionally libraries, for example, while providing the best information, have not attempted to proselytize the information they make available, leaving such matters to government information campaigns. Should this change to assist national development projects?

If we take Bell's analysis of how post-industrial (he later claimed that a post-industrial society is an information society) societies evolve, we must recognize three additional components beyond the general change in the workforce and the accelerated increase in numbers of technologists and engineers. One of these is recognition of an orientation to control the future. This is not as dramatic as it sounds but refers to the need to calculate in advance our needs for power supplies, school and hospital services, housing and so on. Take the provision of electric power as an interesting example. As it takes several years to build electric generating capacity we must have foreknowledge of what generating capacity we need in five or ten years' time. That calculation is now tempered with other considerations. What about global warming? Do we want to be dependent on foreign, and maybe expensive and volatile, supplies of fuel for the generating stations? Are we happy with arguments about the expense, safety, effectiveness and 'greenness' of nuclear power? Are alternative sources of power like wind, wave, tide, geothermal or solar power a realistic proposition? Do claims about 'clean coal' stand up to examination? Are we prepared to make compromises and if so of what kind – forego power-generating capacity, depend on outside fuel supplies, have faith in as-yet undeveloped technologies?

Although these are all political, financial and economic questions, they are also information questions, and there seems to be a need to ensure that the flow of information will effectively allow the best decision making. An information society, now even more than when Daniel Bell was writing, is in need of information as well as creating new information and knowledge.

Another element of the information society identified by Bell is the development of new intellectual technologies. These are needed to assist the decision making about the future. 'New knowledge', as scientific advance, is needed, but just as with the application of new advances in agriculture, there is a body of people, outside scientific research but concerned with its application, who need devices, usually sets of agreed and efficient procedures to effect the process of analysis and decision making. Those people who draw Gannt charts, do critical path analysis, or know about Poisson distributions or stochastic processes are employing a set of intellectual technologies that make decision making a rational rather than an intuitive process.

Some decisions, for example political decisions, are not going to be made with slide rules or by the use of set rules and algorithms, but many more of us need the new intellectual technologies to get the information we need (any web browser search engine is an example) and to help us make the professional decisions that are part of everyday life. Dissemination of this second-order knowledge is critical to life in the information society. Next time you calculate how much weed-killer per square yard or square metre you must put on your garden think about the process that gives you just the right amount. How do you find that information? The answer is that it is on the side of the packet of weed-killer, or you could probably look it up on the net, but was there any decision by anyone that this information must be available, and in what format? Regulators may determine that information on the application of toxic substances, like weed-killer, should be dispensed at the point of sale, but that is a safety decision, or a marketing decision, not a strictly information decision. Information policy is often the offspring of another question. What we assume is that the person using the product is in a position to know that the information provided with the weed-killer is true, or likely to be true. That implies another, educational, decision, which is also an information decision.

Finally, and this is probably the critical information issue, both for information in general and for information policy. Bell claims that in an information society we accept the centrality of theoretical knowledge, and the critically important role of sustaining the mechanisms that make that information available. Those mechanisms include the databases but also the libraries, the information retrieval systems, the indexing rules and so on that allow us all to search and to find. They also allow us to be efficient, to make advances in knowledge that can be widely accepted as certain (reproducible experiments, peer reviewed journals) and not to replicate knowledge or tests of it (rapid dissemination to the wider community of the results).

This claim, which is a claim about the way the world is now, not a prediction about a future state, raises interesting questions for information policy discussions. First, we can ask if any policy initiatives would have any effect on this state of affairs, or has the development that Bell describes happened anyway – in other words, have information policy actions contributed to this outcome, or have they been irrelevant? We can call these the strong and weak theoretical positions to take on information policy, and the implications of them will be developed later. A second question, similar in nature, is to ask if the maintenance of this information society and its dependence on the development and use of knowledge can be sustained whatever information policy actions we might take, or is it dependent on them? To maintain that Bell's analysis is strong we would have to say that information policy is really a consequence of the larger societal developments that have produced the information society. This also implies that the information society is an operating context for information policy and we should understand our policy actions as being conducted within and under the general frame of the information society – in effect that information policy derives its current significance from the information society and only has command of our attention within that general set of arguments about the information society.

In some sense we can see developments over the last decade that obviously support that view. Developments in the regulation of intellectual property seem to reflect the importance of new knowledge and its use. The urgency with which international agreements on intellectual property regulation have been pursued seems to bear out claims that policies naturally follow on from the overall state of the world rather than in any way determining it. Moves to recognize new forms of intellectual property, like databases and computer programs, and to provide special new forms of protection for them also seem to show that policy – in this case in the form of international agreement leading to national regulation – is just a regulatory follow-on from recognizing certain imperatives in the new way the world works.

The information society: alternative views

The claims advanced by Bell about the information society are not universally accepted, and even commentators who are in broad agreement about the importance of information and knowledge in the world and are willing to use the same, or broadly similar, terms to describe it do not always recognize Bell's analysis. In some cases this is because Bell leaves much unexplained, and deeper analysis of how information and knowledge are used in the economy today requires more than Bell gives us. The raw claim that the information sector in society was on track to be the form of employment for the majority was, after some initial optimistic surveys in the 1970s, shown to be unsustainable, but it remained true that information and knowledge industries seemed to be driving economic development. Not all workers in information enterprises were information workers, and many outside the information sector were clearly employed to develop or disseminate new knowledge. No one has claimed that agriculture is an information industry but it employs a lot of information (from weather forecasts to the most complex chemical products), and many people whose business is to use that knowledge.

What was needed, and was supplied by Nico Stehr's work on knowledge societies (1994), was a consideration of the way information has affected more general economic behaviour and has come to be key in non-information businesses. What was previously an unexamined question, that of how information actually transforms businesses and generates wealth, was part of Stehr's inquiry. His examination of what he called the 'black box' of information and knowledge reveals what, from our point of view, is a significant point for information policy.

The two elements of this that contribute to our discussion are, first, the observation that the information classes, those who command the generation and use of knowledge, do not form any new power grouping in society, and are generally in a supportive relationship to existing power groups. Despite the dependence on information for the operation of political and economic power this seems to support a 'weak' theory of information policy, the idea that it follows from other developments in nations rather than determining them. The second point is that businesses and economies become 'smart' using information as intelligence about operating circumstances like markets and trends as well as information as new knowledge to drive the development of new products. This in turn puts high pressure both on a free and rapid access to and flow of information and on the protection of new knowledge as intellectual property. There is an interesting aspect in this last point in that some social products like new financial instruments have no intellectual property protection at all, and there is in effect a free fight over the development of management instruments to finance the development of new products from new scientific knowledge, which does of course have intellectual property protection.

From this we can suggest that a 'weak' theory of information policy will see such policies developing only where they are necessary, perhaps to determine property rights or regulate social behaviour, and that they do not appear at all in other areas either where there is no demand or where markets are thought to operate well without them. In contrast, it is difficult to see what a 'strong' theory of information policy would propose in respect of these different circumstances, and we can merely propose that a strong theory only develops information policy strands where they are necessary, a stance that would leave large areas of information activity outside any information policy framework. This issue we will revisit later, as, from the point of view of developing information policies and strategies, a 'strong' view of policy is methodologically most rewarding and offers the easiest framework for construction. The lack of a strong theory of information policy also makes more difficult the construction of information strategies.

This little complication that a deeper consideration of information policy arguments introduces needs to be set against the fact that theories of the information society do make information central and the role of maintaining, and maintaining access to, knowledge and information critically important, all of which makes for a confident theory of information policy, even if not a strong one. This confidence might be damaged if those claims that deny arguments about information societies were felt to have any validity. Currently, the arguments about our age being an information age, society, economy or whatever are seemingly accepted without examination, and as their appeal is usually to the empirical evidence of observable phenomena their position is not analytically well defended. So, we should give some consideration to the information policy implications of arguments against the idea of an information society.

If we were to accept uncritically the idea that we live in an information society we might be surrendering some of the power that flows to information policies if those claims were to be false or to become displaced. For, whether the information society idea allows us a strong or a weak conception of information policy, it does seem to offer a very convenient general framework for information policies. Actually, some interesting possibilities open up if the information society idea is not sustainable because, although that situation does not automatically invalidate claims about the strength of information policies it does allow us to conceive of information policies as being more autonomous than we might otherwise have to accept. For the moment we need to consider three strong claims that the claims about the information society are not justifiable.

First, we might briefly consider a pseudo-Marxist position that would claim, as Touraine did in his book *The Post-Industrial Society* (1971), that the information society idea is really just a description of a late stage of capitalism, that the standard Marxist claims about the eventual, indeed imminent, collapse of capitalism still stand good, and that in consequence we would have to accept that the range of information policies normally discussed were just part of the superstructure of capitalist society, designed to maintain the control of the dominant class over the means of intellectual production, distribution and exchange. However, two points stand out: first, despite the best efforts of many bankers over the last 18 months or so, capitalism has not collapsed and we can say that whatever the arguments deployed about the ultimate role or purpose of information policies notions about the political order are outside our control. We still need to consider how we attempt to regulate or offer guidance on the generation and flow of information in the situation we happen to be in, and information policies as we normally consider them have the same role to play as they have done in the last 20 years or so. The claim that if we were true proletarians intent on advancing the inevitable socialist revolution (a claim that has not been heard much recently) we should be advancing information policies that would help bring that about is really, in the terms we have discussed above, an argument for a 'strong' theory of information policy. The second point about Marxist claims is that, as indicated, we don't hear much about them these days and even if they did supply good arguments we might want a more secure foundation for our claims about the nature of policy and a more convincing analysis of how to formulate policy.

A second set of arguments that deny many of the claims put forward about the information society can be associated with the idea that the phenomena collectively labelled the information society did indeed happen but they are not so significant a change as has been claimed and are in fact just a continuation of industrial society. Sometimes labelled the control revolution these arguments centre attention on the increased power of scrutiny over all aspects of work, and indeed social life, that computer power has brought. For these claims we can simply say that the position of information policies does not change: they are still important – indeed, as part of the mechanisms of control they are more important – but that they really fall into place as the servant of other needs, and in this way we would have to accept a 'weak' theory of information policy, whereby such policies, however effective they might be, were not initiators or determinants of changes in economic, social or political life and were just employed, as needed, to bring about results determined by discussions about other things. The other point to make here is that such information policies would just go on and on, changed when debate desired, and would not stand or fall with any overarching theory of what society was about or what analysis of the age we currently favour.

A final set of arguments that form an alternative to the information society claims are those that deny the existence of the information society, describe the information society phenomena as evidence of a deterioration of the human condition, and call for some effort to transcend the current state of life and reassert the human values that constitute the essential nature of mankind. These claims are reactions to the organizational revolution of the last century or so, the developments in the management of human life that allow us to live in large cities with complex work, transportation, educational and health systems, but require that we subordinate ourselves to the discipline of social organization to do so. Adherents of this position decry the imposition of the complex social systems that deliver education and so on to us, claiming that 'real' education, or whatever, would be tailored to individual need and circumstance, rather than putting us through packaged systems that we have come to accept without question. For people who argue that we endure these encroachments on human freedom and that we are in effect all reduced to the level of machines within organizations the salvation lies in a different, perhaps more spiritual, but certainly more idealized form of human existence in which access to information for services that would fill individual need would be critically important. For information policy we could say again that a 'strong' theory of information policies would not fit, and that information policies could not have any autonomy, being required to be part of the general social policies that realized the enhanced human condition.

However, it has to be said of all these theories that centre on the idea of the information society that access to information is critical for all of them, and in that sense we have the foundation for a set of information policies that work within all the different analyses discussed above. How strong and weak theories of information policy work in other conceptions of modern life needs our consideration, too, and immediately we should review arguments about the development of a public sphere, for these would seem to require most obviously a strong theory of information policy.

3
Information policy and the public sphere

DISCUSSION OF THE information society idea and information policy gave us the idea about weak and strong theories of information policy, and also the ideas of autonomy for information policy and the operational frameworks for them. The idea of the public sphere is so closely identified with the exchange of information and the rules governing it that information policy must seem either redundant, because the public sphere is a socially and historically determined environment that itself constitutes the rules for information exchange, or it must seem that the public sphere legitimates a regime of information policy to sustain its existence. This divergence we will unravel later. At present we just need to identify some of the characteristics of the public sphere and some of the arguments about its nature.

We are all familiar with public discussion of topical issues, be they international or national political questions, the world economy, questions of social norms and expectations, or disease, war, education – in fact all the issues of modern life. We are also used to ceaseless coverage of leisure activities in the media – sport, music, films, even books, and the lives of celebrities. Many of us are now also daily consumers of more private information that we individually put into a public arena, or make publicly accessible, through social networking media like Facebook, Twitter and so on. This volume of publicly accessible information is a recent phenomenon that poses and faces several threats. One threat, mentioned in Chapter 1, is to personal privacy as we disclose so much about ourselves. Another more recent potential threat is to the existence of the institutional forms through which we are accustomed to getting our public discussions – the serious newspapers and television programmes. Many of these depend on advertising revenue and now face closure as two forces combine to assail their revenue. First, the current economic downturn, which is diminishing advertising budgets and revenues, and this is escalating the impact of, second, a more long term decline in advertising as many staple sources of small town and national newspapers find alternative and cheaper ways to advertise through the internet. Strange as it may seem now, the forces that controlled advertising have been identified by the major author of ideas about the public sphere as the primary cause of corruption in the public sphere.

As we face a possible strategic change in the way public discussion is sustained it would be interesting to know whether that 'corruption' is to be corrected, maybe through the internet, or whether we will have to pay a higher price for our public arenas of ideas and debate. It might seem that this is an obvious occasion to use information policies to sustain the kind of public sphere that we want, extending information policy to include direct intervention in print media through public subsidy or even publicly financing competing public service broadcasting services. We should ask whether such action would ossify natural development or sustain the institutional infrastructure of society, and that question should prompt inquiry into what constitutes the public sphere and whether there are alternatives.

The idea of a public sphere

Jurgen Habermas is usually credited as the originating author of the idea of a public sphere, although Reinhart Koselleck (1988[1959]) had proposed the concept slightly earlier. Habermas's work appeared first in

German in 1962, was translated into French in 1979, and appeared in English translation, as *The Structural Transformation of the Bourgeois Public Sphere* only in 1989. The debate in the English speaking world about the public sphere thus began much later than in other parts of Europe. The ideas put forward by Habermas aroused much comment and further study, including extensive consideration of the impact of the idea of publicity on aspects of social life. Broadly speaking, the effect of increased publicity is to extend public involvement into areas of life that hitherto escaped comment or regulation. We are so familiar with this that it passes without comment: publicity is the spur to campaigns and action, whether on matters of child safety, crime or banking practices. The structure of action whereby public attention is engaged by campaigning groups through media exposure, and then public pressure mounts for some action, law or change of practice, is one so common that we give it no thought.

Two recent events in Britain illustrate the practice that we accept as normal. First, in 2008, a baby died through neglect and ill treatment, despite the involvement of the Social Services Department of the local authority. A public enquiry itemized the treatment of the child and the failures of the various public services that failed to identify the risk to the child. We might formerly have thought that the activity of a family in its child-rearing practices was not an area of public interest and would be disturbed at the suggestion that the public had a right to inquire into the way we care for our own children: this is an aspect of private family life. Yet we concur that public intrusion in this particular case (the case of Baby P) is correct: the public sphere extends to the interests of the child.

The second case, in 2009, concerned the public exposure of certain expenses claims made by British members of parliament. Concern at these expenses had been growing for some time, and the parliamentarians' own investigation, under the leadership of the Speaker of the House of Commons, had been proceeding very slowly. Eventually a document itemising the expenses claims, and identifying the MPs making them, was passed by a civil servant to the *Daily Telegraph* and the details were published, leading to the resignation of some MPs and the dismissal of some ministers in the government. Later, the parliamentarians' own report on their expenses claims was released: it concealed details of the MPs' residences and details of certain payments. Some MPs even claimed that no information about where they lived should be released to the public because it might jeopardize their safety and that of their families. The public exposure of the expenses and the risible, scandalous or pitiful claims being made was very entertaining for the public and was deemed a legitimate public interest. The civil servant who leaked the information did so 'in the public interest'. Despite this being a breach of his conditions of employment no action was taken against him.

As in the Baby P case, the exposure of the information was considered a legitimate extension of the public sphere, as taxpayers' money and the conduct of elected representatives was at issue. Yet, just as the way families raise their children might be considered private, this issue could be considered, as some MPs apparently wished it to be, as a secret of the state. If we turn back the clock several hundred years we can find different conditions operating, so Habermas claims. In the mediaeval state the king, literally, represented the state, and his business was the business of state. No public sphere of exposure of information existed: those matters proper to the domestic and private life of households were not made public, and anyone working for the state was working for the king and kept his business private. To do otherwise could have been considered treason. To oppose, or even publicly doubt, the king's actions was an act of rebellion. Of course, there was public life, and probably local talk about harvests, fairs, markets, crime, plagues, justice, taxes and so on, but nothing like the degree of public debate we accept today. That came about slowly as first merchants and then others began to gather and exchange information that was not state information but was necessarily made public through coffee house chat and then published broadsheets and finally in newspapers. Even officially illegal reporting of the debates in the British House of Commons was tolerated by the mid-18th century and gradually the publication of an accurate record

of parliamentary debates became a key part of the apparatus of democratic society.

We can imagine that the information that merchants needed to
exchange about the arrival of ships, news of harvests, wars, diseases,
the availability of products and markets, and price information would
have been traded in an open manner. This incipient public sphere would
have needed uncorrupted information, the best available. Of course,
such discussions, though initially on economic matters, would have
included political information about foreign states and would also have
touched on matters like taxation at home. Gradually more and more of
the business of the state would have come under discussion, and it
would have been part of a wider exchange of information and views about
economic and social matters. As the balance of wealth between the
monarch and some members of the public began to change the monarch
ceased to be the only provider of public entertainment and the court was
no longer the only source of social gatherings. The public sphere was
born, the precursor of the huge media and information industries we
have today.

According to Habermas, the public sphere first appeared in England
in the later 17th century, and by the next century was known in France,
Prussia, the Low Countries and other advanced parts of Europe. Even
repressive regimes were not able to suppress public discussion of a
widening range of issues. That discussion was not among the mass
public who today tune in to TV programmes every night and buy
tabloid newspapers. The circle of debate was limited to elites, not merely
aristocratic but not extending beyond educated classes of some wealth
and social standing. Habermas's claim is that in the 18th and up until
the early 19th century there was an idealized and almost perfect public sphere of discussion, where the range of issues and the quality of
information exchanged was not corrupted by interests other than those
of the people concerned to get access to, and contribute to, the best
knowledge available.

There are two points to note here. First, as you open your daily newspaper, even if it is not aimed at a mass market, you may find it contains more than necessary intelligence to aid decision making about current issues. Second, you would most likely have made no contribution to any debates or discussions it contains, and there may be no obvious means for you to do so. There are opportunities to participate with the mass media – you can write for tickets for studio performances or discussion programmes, you can write letters to the editors of newspapers, or enter competitions they run, but by and large your participation is limited to the form determined by the programme makers or newspaper editors or owners. Of course, if you don't like the TV programmes you can switch off, or over to another channel, or you can buy a different newspaper. The point is that the form of engagement lacks reciprocity; it is not an opportunity for equal exchange, or determination between equals of the format. Consumption of the mass media is just that, consumption of another product. Habermas maintains therefore that the form in which public sphere debate is sustained has changed, as it has gone through a structural transformation, which has been detrimental to its character. We may not feel it to be detrimental and we may have adjusted to operate within the form in which it is made available to us, but something has been lost, even though there is a gain for those readers and viewers in the mass public who have some level of observer status in the public sphere opened up to them.

The structure of the public sphere

We need to clarify some information policy issues in this area, and to start a debate about the relationship between various information policy mechanisms and instruments, the intentions we might have about the public sphere, and the possibilities for understanding the role of information policy in the structuring of the public sphere. It is obvious that much of what can be said, much of what may be reported, and the way in which ownership of media products is determined all affect the way the public sphere can operate.

One other point, not related directly to information policy, needs to be introduced here. It can be claimed that the continued pressure for publicly available information has opened up more aspects of life to public scrutiny than was previously true. While the public sphere grew and intruded into the private and the secret state spheres, it is also true that increased public exposure in the public sphere, through media coverage, has improved, or at least has led to hopes for improvement, in the lot of those who otherwise were disadvantaged or repressed. A current example was given above in the Baby P case; a more general one would be the coverage given to slavery, and more recently to the garment workers producing cheap goods for western markets who have to work in unsatisfactory and sometimes unsafe conditions for long hours and low pay. The exposure of exploitation may lead to improvement in their working lives. In these cases the loss of privacy (a value information policy might seek to protect) is balanced by a greater good. So, it is possible that objectives of information policy, in this case privacy, might have to give way to achieve other ends that, although not information policy issues, depend on the use of information: we might be supporting an information policy that allows common values to be relegated.

In this instance the balance between privacy and free access to information is swayed by non-information considerations. The play of information policies, in particular censorship, privacy and freedom of information, would seem to be absolutely critical for the maintenance of the public sphere. We might become confused here by the sense that apparently ideas about the public sphere must require a strong theory of information policies, and a strongly autonomous range of information policies, but we need to drill down further into this question. Habermas's public sphere, although stemming from his analysis of empirical conditions, is an idealized construct, the characteristics of which we will examine shortly. We can accept without comment his observation of the historical forces that shaped the public sphere but ask if now we are faced with a principle of publicity that demands certain types of information policies in order to sustain the operation of the public sphere.

An alternative view would say the public sphere is merely a consequence of the interplay of other powerful forces, such as financial power and new technology, and that information policies are merely incidental. Let us look at a couple of other empirical examples that may clarify this point. The example given above about the expenses of British parliamentarians came at a time when the possibility of a privacy law was under discussion (for entirely different reasons). Such a law would have made impossible the kinds of disclosure that entertained the public for several weeks early in 2009. Those exposures were felt to be a greater good than the privacy of parliamentarians (and, incidentally, of ordinary members of the general public), the chances of a privacy law receded from the political agenda, and the idea of the beneficial reach of the public sphere was sustained.

Here the political idea of public exposure worked to influence the way information policies would be deployed, and, as we saw with the case of arguments about the information society, we must assume that only a weak theory of information policy will properly describe how they operate. Central to this question of parliamentary expenses was the sense of public outrage that would surface when the character, range and amount of these expenses emerged. The sense of publicity here is not like the notional 18th-century public sphere where information is exchanged between equals to benefit discussion and the advance of knowledge, but rather an appeal to mass shock and disapproval, with no sense that the mass reading public would be involved in discussion about the issue.

At the other end of the spectrum, but still staying with questions of privacy, a celebrated model was photographed outside a rehabilitation clinic and the photo published in a national newspaper and an accompanying newspaper article reminded readers of the model's public stance on drug taking and dependence. Was her privacy invaded? Was the public interest served by publicizing the seeming contradiction between her statements and her apparent behaviour? Lower courts held that the public interest was served, but the higher court upheld her claims about her privacy. The publicity, again, was not to engage the mass public in discussion but to maximize the exposure to censure for a person dependent on a positive public image.

There are several complications in this story. First, it is often held, but not explained or described in any way that could be legislated, that people who openly lead lives in the public gaze cannot expect to have the same level of privacy protection that an ordinary citizen might claim. In the case of the expenses of parliamentarians we saw that principle in action. In the USA the contradiction between statements on illegal immigrants that conflict with the employment practices of certain political figures has also been exposed, and the argument that the public good is better served by the exposure than the protection of the politicians' (and their employees') privacy seems to be accepted. Second, we can accept that statements about some things have to come from certain people, but a statement about drug taking could be made by anyone and the message would have the same intellectual content even if it would be less forcefully conveyed than it would by a more famous person. The message can be separated from the messenger.

In the case of the model it would seem that there is no strong public interest point to be made, whatever the courts' decisions might be. Whatever we may think about what the model deserved, the operation of the current state of law in privacy in England is not an issue closely connected to maintaining the public sphere and the need to inquire into and report on all matters that need public debate and action. This must lead us to suppose that there is no exact match between ideas about the public sphere and ideas about privacy. We could find other examples, pertaining to intellectual property for example, that would amplify the same point. These examples show that information policy is autonomous in its relation to the public sphere, even though public sphere arguments must depend on the operation of information policies in several areas to maintain the access to and exchange of information.

The character of the public sphere

Another question must relate to the exact character of the public sphere. If it has undergone structural transformation following the paramountcy of capitalist interests in the media then we must wonder what sustains the sphere and, if the character has changed, whether various information policies must also have changed. At this point we should agree that various mechanisms for sustaining Habermas' ideal public sphere, although effective in governing the way information is exchanged, are not in themselves information policies. For example, the provision that the exchange of knowledge and information should be on a basis of reciprocity between the agents, where all participants meet as equals, whatever their relative status in other forms of life, is a social provision, not an information provision. Information policies cannot determine the character of the public sphere or the character of the exchange of information – for example, whether the exchange is equal. For example, although rules about the use of intellectual property may be used to determine that the rights of all parties are respected, they cannot determine the nature of every market transaction. General notions that inform information policy decisions, like the idea of improved access to information, can set the tone but they cannot guarantee delivery. Explicit provisions about censorship or secrecy, although they may be respected in the main, cannot always be guaranteed either, as the example of the MPs' expenses showed. There is a 'black box' (in the sense of an unexamined and poorly understood mechanism) circularity in this matter: information policies do specify how information will be transferred, both privately and in the public sphere, but the way the general public interest works will determine just when those information policy provisions will be applied or when they will be ignored.

To bring this out more clearly we can discuss aspects of some other ideas about the public sphere. One claim is that the idealized public sphere given to us by Habermas is but one of a range of possible public spheres, which differ in character. Villa (1992, 712) summarizes the Habermasian public sphere as 'a specifically political space distinct from the state and the economy, an institutionally bounded discursive arena that is home to citizen debate, deliberation, agreement, and action'. Characteristic of this are:

- agreement about equality
- symmetry
- an absence of hierarchy
- the idea that we operate in this space as equals
- no coercive force
- the possibility of consensus and joint action as the source of power, in which we all have the possibility of power.

This is a strongly associational concept of the public sphere, where no action is taken without all participants being consulted and no course being pursued that is not consensual. It may be ideal but it fails to recognize realities of existence, the most obvious of which is that power does exist and it is exercised on us. One account justifying the idea of the public sphere would say that establishing, recognizing and maintaining a public sphere is the surest means we have to protect ourselves against the use of power against us, but that we should be realistic about the real nature of that sphere. The characteristics of the Habermasian public sphere rest legitimacy for action in its consensual and associational nature: alternative analyses offer different foundations for legitimacy. One such would be what has been labelled by Benhabib (1992) the liberal–juridical public sphere, sometimes called the Kantian public sphere. In this the following would be characteristic:

- The paramount issue is legitimacy.
- The framework is legalistic.
- Discourse is characterized by legalism.
- It aims at a Kantian 'just and stable public order'.

This is probably close to the public sphere of international organizations and treaty negotiations, and also of many national government processes, and the legalistic framework works to secure an agreed operating format that minimizes or manages dispute regulation and secures some level of politeness in information exchange, so we have laws against incitement to religious hatred, libel and slander, and with information rights we find that all, potentially, may be curtailed by the demands of maintaining public order. In this environment information policies work as legal instruments and they may, as with intellectual property laws, be used as a basis for dispute regulation rather than as instruments for securing consensus. But that is a comment on how the law is used; it is not clear that such laws would change if we did have a Habermasian associational public sphere – we would just use the same law but in a different way.

Hannah Arendt has proposed a more radically different idea of public space where the individual members use the space as a stage to compete for attention and fame rather than as an arena to negotiate consensus. Such a view of the public sphere would:

- emphasize the agonistic aspect of public space: the idea is of a competitive public space
- be a place where we compete for recognition
- identify the task as to escape the futility of existence by acting to achieve some immortality in the minds of society
- not be a consensus making, associational sphere
- have the attraction of immediacy, spontaneity and participation
- not be procedural
- assume an egalitarian, homogeneous society.

In such a world all the questions about association have already been answered. The pursuit or exercise of power is not a question for the competitive members, for the power in such a society lies elsewhere with a physically or socially remote sovereign who reserves political power unless it is seized by others.

Here information policy has the role of setting the boundaries of legitimate action within which the members compete. The goal is fame, not agreement. In this context information policies are autonomous; they are not produced by this idea of a public sphere but they are employed by such a sphere to enable its actions. In this discussion we can assume that we need a strong theory of information policies, for they must have power to compel behaviour if their role as a rule maker is to work. The basis for such a 'strong' theory needs to become apparent. What set of principles would enable us to develop a theory of what information policy should be, how it should operate, and what its effects should be?

This poses another set of questions, because our discussion has shown that in certain understandings of what the information society, or the public sphere, is, we can have only a 'weak' theory of information policy. Do we then need a set of frameworks for information policy that allow us to construct strong or weak theories as we need them? An alternative would be a set of arguments that allowed us to construct a view of information policy that would operate in any of the circumstances we have discussed, that would allow, and enable the development of, further weapons in the armoury of information policies beyond those commonly understood today, and would have consciousness of the effects of various information policy instruments, both singly and in combination. It would also have to allow the use of such policies in the varying circumstances that demand weak or strong theories of information policy.

This is a tall order. It means we should be very confident about what information policies may or can do, and that we should be able to say that if a certain mix of information policies will operate in a way that we can identify as strong or weak. How important for us, then, is it that we can say whether something is strong or weak? We can recall that strong information policy theories will operate on our public sphere or in our information society to bring about certain results and determine the character of that society or sphere. Weak theories, on the other hand, are unable to shape the information society or public sphere, and are in fact determined in their character and effect by them.

The discussion now needs to consider two other influencing factors. The first, which we can discuss briefly as an incipient new version of the public sphere, is the internet. This is interesting as a potential example of Habermas's associational public sphere, free of coercion or control, and establishing consensus through voluntary memberships. The second, which we will treat as a separate chapter, are those information rights established through international treaties and conventions and which offer us some basis for identifying a framework for an overall view of information policy and its imperatives.

The internet has since 1993 established itself as an almost essential component of the work and lives of a vast number of people. For some it is an essential tool for work, for others a convenience for work, and for still more it is a source of entertainment or social contact. Typically through the world wide web, but also through other access points, we can get access to vast amounts of information, which we can read, download for use, or change and transmit. In this new public sphere:

- all the information controls that operate in the print sphere can be found
- but these networks also have other characteristics not entirely covered by the information rules of the print sphere
- some actors may be cut out of the loop if they do not have access to the technology, or lack the means to use it.

The internet could be, fleetingly, free of the kinds of controls that typically are found in terrestrial societies and jurisdictions. This may change as various regimes seek to control access. For example, it is illegal to sell Nazi memorabilia in Germany, so some items available on online auction sites might offend German law and the German authorities might seek to prohibit access to such material, which could be done by putting pressure on the internet service providers. Such was the action taken by the Chinese authorities when they wished to silence criticism of their regime at the time of the Beijing Olympic Games: major providers apparently colluded with the Chinese government in this matter. France and Australia have passed laws that effectively extend their jurisdiction to the terrestrial base of whatever internet sites they object to. (All internet material must be hosted on a computer that will be somewhere on earth, or in a satellite that comes under the jurisdiction of a nation state or international law.)

We can recall that Habermas objected to the corruption of the ideal bourgeois public sphere, typically by commercial interests but especially by electronic media. The internet must count as electronic media, so how is it financed? Advertising, and the sale of access to expensive sites, seem to be major sources of revenue, but also much material is made available *pro bono publico* and effectively paid for by governments or taxpayers. Habermas wrote of a 'political public sphere characterized by at least two crosscutting processes: the communicative generation of legitimate power on the one hand and the manipulative deployment of media power to procure mass loyalty, consumer demand, and "compliance" with systemic imperatives on the other' (1993, 452).

So far there is little evidence of the internet being used for the 'communicative generation of legitimate power', but two examples might indicate how this will change. First, the effective use of the internet and particularly its social networking software facilities (sometimes called Web 2.0) by Barack Obama in his campaign for the American presidency in 2008 could be seen, according to your point of view, as the generation of legitimate power or corruption by media manipulation. Second, the attempts to generate internet protests against various governments worldwide for their treatment of sections of their own populations, attempts that are usually blocked by the countries concerned, can be seen as an obvious attempt to generate legitimate political power.

Information policies about the internet so far show little sign of effective adaptation to the new medium. Laws on intellectual property are frequently broken and attempts at controlling, say, the pirating of music by internet sites has proved to be a limited success. Laws on censorship are easily broken in western countries and even in other regimes effective censorship is maintained by controlling access to the medium by readers rather than by those who generate the information. Governments have used the internet very effectively to give improved access to vast quantities of information that would be difficult to print or make easily available by other means, and so are giving effect to freedom of information campaigns, but the internet does not force governments to disclose information and no information policy can force that either, except by national legislation or international treaty obligation. Privacy and data protection legislation can easily be broken by internet communication, and carelessness by government agents in several countries has allowed the disclosure of the health, personal and financial information of millions of their citizens. The internet, and international data transmission, is an area of weakness for data security, making identity theft and subsequent fraudulent activity easier.

So, for the internet we have to accept that only a weak theory of information policy can be proposed, information policies do not change the character of how the internet works, and the extra pressures that the internet creates over data security may weaken even further the effect of information policy. Strangely, that very weakness might actually lead to action at a level below that of the nation state, as parents and citizen groups seek to control access to what may be seen over the internet by installing filter software, educating their children, or combining with others to put pressure on internet service providers. This would swing the balance of control over information policies away from national legislatures and towards other groups, but as these would lack legitimate political power and be acting as consumers it would seem that any such movement could not be very extensive or effective over whole jurisdictions. To see what other powers citizens may have over information policy we will look at the question of information rights, after a brief consideration of the situation where there is no acceptance of claims about either an information society or a public sphere.

Epilogue to Chapter 3

If claims about the information society and the public sphere are rejected, or at least if any claims they may have to influence information policy are rejected, then such policies must be seen in a new light. It only makes sense if we reject all claims of overarching theories of society to subordinate information policy, for otherwise we would be trying to anticipate large scale social explanations which as yet have no explicit form. To the argument that post-modernist theories would allow any multiplicity of information policies to be in force without us being able either to make claims about them or to make any statement about their role within any version or explanation of social forces, we have no comment to make, for the post-modernist claimant seems to be saying that there is a name for modern social movements, post-modernism, but that it can be held to make no overarching claims. We are with this position exactly where we are with the idea that there are no overarching explanations for modern social change.

A final set of comments relates to the situation where there is a substantial claim for the existence of an information society or a public sphere but that analysis shows information policies to have no effect in relation to them. Should we then discount information policies? The answer is no, because they will have been brought into existence, or will remain as conventional practice, in order to accomplish some more limited objective that no other convenient practice or law can encompass – in other words, they have a local validity, and may have some substantial efficacy, even if they are not a formal part of a more general social process in which they are swept along. Censorship as a recourse of governments seems to have a sustained existence independently of any economic or social analysis, and although it may not formally contribute to the development of any grand theory of social change it seems to justify study as a long-lived device for control of what people read, distribute and view. We have several grounds to study and analyse information policies, with and without the high level grand theories about information societies and public spheres, but we should also retain a readiness to be aware of the role of information policies within these should there be grounds to believe they occur.

We put forward the argument that there would have to be a strong theory of information policy if it was independent of any named large social change but also had the effect of bringing that change about – in other words, that it has causal power beyond the explicit intentions of a piece of legislation or government policy. It was also argued that a weak theory of information policy should be seen when policies were entirely subordinate to the social movement that brought them into existence. We have also said that information policies are autonomous when they have some existence independent of the view of information society or public sphere they are held to be a supportive part of, and may continue in existence even if those grand claims are rejected or superseded.

All these statements relate to information policies put into effect as the conscious intention of a government or legislature for a nation or other jurisdiction. A different situation holds when information policies either emerge spontaneously or are the product of non-governmental social movements, but when we speak of these we must be careful to distinguish what can be counted as an information policy from what is just a consumer choice, especially when the latter is the product of technological change. For example, most governments now have policies to encourage internet use, both socially and educationally, to use internet access to improve access to government information, and sometimes to encourage political participation. As part of all this they encourage, support, legislate for and sometimes fund provision of broadband access. Yet when the internet first appeared its use seemed to depend on a combination of technological advance providing capacity, industry self-regulation developing the necessary protocols, and consumer choice. The involvement of governments and media industries came soon after but it is not clear that current intentional policy was a precondition for mass consumer preference.

Where particular policies are followed independently of governments quite clearly the policies must be considered strong, but it is not clear that they represent a strong theory of information policy – they are just effective demonstrations of citizen decision making. Should we then say that where national governments or their agencies do not take a lead in information policy that we should be talking about a weak theory of information policy? It does not seem to matter, because when we speak of weak or strong theories we are talking about our analysis of the information policy situation, we are not talking about the effects of those policies or the idea of information policy in any one jurisdiction. Discussion of a weak or strong theory must relate not to an account of what happens but to our overall understanding of information policy.

So, to return to the question posed at the start of this section, what to say about information policies where there is no grand theory of society or its communication space, we can for the moment dispense with ideas about weak or strong theories, but we should not dismiss notions of the autonomy of information policies. This may become more apparent when we discuss information rights, but a brief elaboration here will prepare some of the ground for that. When a particular piece of legislation provides a remedy for some situation not every effect of that legislation or the character of its application can be foreseen.

A striking example is the British Official Secrets Act of 1911. This act, very simply worded, was passed through all its parliamentary stages (six readings) in one afternoon, in a state of political panic. It proved to be very effective, more so than the most secretive of public servants can have imagined, so much so that not only were its provisions for nearly a century a stumbling block in Britain for any easing of official secrecy but the simplicity of its wording proved very difficult to better, thus serving to deflect attempts to weaken its provisions. Exceptions to the general rule of secrecy it introduced depended on authorisation, without making clear who had the power to authorize such relaxations. More recently, a very complex and lengthy series of international negotiations about intellectual property rights has produced a regime that, in hindsight, may seem to some to favour producers more than consumers, and there may be a growing feeling now that the balance needs to swing a little the other way. These examples show that policies, even at the most general level and in the wording of single laws, may demonstrate autonomy in action, either through inertia or by empowering certain parties to agreements, that was not originally intended. The provisions in national legislation and international agreements setting out information rights can be seen in the same way, particularly in the caveats accompanying them.

4

Information rights and information policy

INFORMATION POLICY AS an issue of rights raises a completely different set of questions that lie outside the framework we have so far considered. Until now we have looked at information policies as parts of larger social forces and movements or as things that stand on their own within the structure of each society. If we look at rights we find that the standard statements about human rights include certain items that we can identify as information rights. No one has looked at information rights independently of other rights and it is not clear that a distinction between various sorts of rights can be made in that way. For example, most statements of rights include a right to freedom of religious belief or practice. This must include, for those religions that use them, the right to use their particular sacred documents. So is freedom of religion an information right? Most people would consider it as a sort of right that stood on its own rather than being one of a group of other rights.

There is also the separate question of how we treat religious claims to the unquestionable status of their own central documents – mostly we do not privilege documents or their contents, so are we inventing a privileged status for religious documents, and does that status subtend from currently practised religions only – in other words is it dependent on the existence of living practitioners – or are all religious documents of all known religions past and present included? If we extend the notion of what counts as a document to include various artefacts with reli-gious or other significance we find that the idea of rights must become very extensive. Commonly rights, especially when expressed as human rights, are held to exist for living humans, and the rights associated with them are cited as rights for any human who happens to be living. So, the right to freedom of expression must exist even if no human being is currently seeking to exercise that right, as must the right to privacy and the right to have certain sorts of information – for example, the right to know of any charges brought against you, and the right to know who your accusers are. These are rights about information too.

We might also want to ask if the information rights, if we could iden-tify them with universal agreement, can be considered to be a complete statement of the information rights that a human being might justifiably claim, or are they just a subset of general rights that exist only in the con-text of rights in general? (It will probably be easier if we discuss rights as one group, rather than trying to disentangle human rights, civic rights, political rights, social rights and so on, and it will certainly be easier to avoid entangling this discussion with claims about a right to education, a right to know, or a right to access the internet.) Here we want to dis-cuss rights in information as part of an approach to information policy that privileges the individual and pivots discussion of information pol-icy around the individual.

What value can lie in that approach? At a simple level we can say that these individual information rights exist and are often directly related to information policy instruments – the right to privacy for example. However, there must be a reason why the information rights exist. One account would centre rights on what the individual needs to flourish as a human being. Others might claim either that the individual needs these rights to be able to operate as an autonomous citizen participat-ing in a democratic society, or that such societies need their members to be able to participate in social and political life in a way that can only be secured by the exercise of these rights which would otherwise be under threat if they were not secured. This last point gives a further hint about the value of looking at information policy as a rights issue. If the things secured by information policies – for example the balance that most societies seek to strike over what should be censored and what should not – are under threat from those with power (see earlier discussions about the public sphere), then understanding them as a necessary right for human functioning gives them a purpose that enables the legislator to work towards the right balance.

If there is no such overarching sense of what any legislation is trying to achieve, then we can see two obvious consequences: the form of legislation will probably only reflect who has power in any society, and it would be very difficult to look at them as policy – something that was intentionally being followed to achieve a particular result. Looking at information rights as a foundation for information policy may help secure the capability of citizens to function autonomously within the society, but it will also allow examination of what information policies are for, what their intended consequences are.

This last suggests, in line with earlier comments, that our understanding of what information rights exist may not be coterminous with those rights itemized in international rights documents. It might be possible in a fuller discussion of information rights to determine an extensive array of rights that no law or no international campaign or treaty yet recognizes. In that spirit we should not limit discussion of the information rights that do exist but extend the coverage to include those that might be useful to achieve certain ends. The point of saying all this is to claim that a rights-based approach to information policy does presuppose some social or political objectives and thus can be seen alongside ideas about the information society or the public sphere as a basis for policy. However, that approach has certain drawbacks.

We can identify three separate objections that we should cover before moving to any itemization of information rights. First, there is a counter claim, as mentioned in Chapter 1, that information policy should work for the government, for business or for some abstract notion of common good, and not just for individuals, and so we should regard rights as not just for individuals but also for other interests. Second, there is the claim that universal human rights just don't exist. Jeremy Bentham (1748–1832) dismissed talk of human rights as 'nonsense upon stilts' and a more recent book by Jeremy Waldron (1987) used that quotation as a title for his refutation of that claim (and those of Edmund Burke and Karl Marx). Third, there is the claim that, whatever international treaties may say, rights are an indulgence that can only be accommodated in good times and at other times most likely will be in abeyance, and meanwhile there must still be information policies to deal with censorship, intellectual property issues or privacy matters, so talk of rights cannot serve as a basis for policy.

The rights of government

The counter claim that information policy should serve business or government is largely consistent with claims for human information rights. We can say that if government is democratic then it will be consistent with recognizing human rights, including information rights. There are three types of cases to consider. First, where in the normal course of events the information rights of individuals may be in conflict with government interests. Second, the case where sovereignty lies with a restricted subset of the population and government extends rights to individuals as a courtesy but overrides them in its own interests, and third, where governments and their agents seek to protect themselves against criticism or removal from office by restricting information rights.

There are occasions when the interests of government will demand higher levels of censorship, and in times of emergency even in democratic societies there may be widespread censorship with some level of general consent. Wartime is an obvious example. Even in normal times there is general recognition that a level of secrecy must surround certain government actions, such as treaty negotiations, defence arrangements, financial planning and contracts for government-funded projects. Freedom of information provisions are recent and have not been tested in wartime, but we can instance the USA PATRIOT Act as an example of a democratic society tolerating very strong curtailments of a wide range of normal checks and balances, reduction in the public provision of state held information, and a sweeping aside of normal privacy provisions. A recent request for information about the involvement of British agents in the 'rendition' process of two people suspected of terrorist associations and intentions was refused by the British government on the grounds it would breach the privacy protection for the individuals concerned. In addition to enhanced censorship and reduced freedom of information there may also be restrictions on freedom of speech. Whether these breach human rights in the interests of protecting the government is debateable. We already accept restrictions on freedom of speech in the interests of not stirring up race or religious hatred. Extensions of these provisions to ensure the preservation of public order do not seem onerous when the case is obvious. The argument here is that individual freedoms can be curtailed in the interests of preserving freedoms for all.

There are two cases where the arguments in favour of governments are not so clearly acceptable. A democratic society, even in times of emergency, must have provision for criticizing government actions and intentions. If the rights of citizens to protest and to criticize are removed merely to aid a government's political survival we feel some rule has been transgressed. The point here is that democratic societies operate with recognized principles, which are given effect by the development and implementation of rules. Where the rules can be seen to represent a principle they are accepted; where they represent merely the abuse of power they are seen as unacceptable. The principles are often given effect as rules about rights. The second point where government restrictions of information rights is seen as unacceptable is when the interests of the public service and its control of political power take precedence over citizens' interests and are used to suppress or override rights.

These cases cover the instances where governments might override rights, but we must also address the case where citizens' rights are seen as secondary to, and subordinate to, government interests. This relates to issues of sovereignty. Where sovereignty lies with the people the issue is clear; where it lies with either a parliament or another sovereign, like a monarch, government interests (when government operates in the interests of the sovereign) might legitimately override individual rights. Even if sovereignty lies with the people if there is some explicit or tacit national project (like victory in war, or national economic development) then government interests might override rights with tacit consent. But it is not clear that government objectives can be realized simply by subordinating rights, and in cases where the inefficient, careless, illegal or abusive actions of government agents or agencies are protected by subordinating individual rights then government efficiency and constitutional propriety are served, alongside the interests of citizens, by zealously protecting and implementing rights, including information rights.

The interests of business

Where there are business projects, particularly if there is some national economic project to develop the economy, the subordination of information rights might seem to be in some collective interest. Notions of the ownership of intellectual property, for example, were very different in the Soviet Union from those that hold almost universally now. Intellectual productivity was rewarded in different ways. Now, almost universally, intellectual property is rewarded by whatever the market will pay, and (as we will see later) it is not clear that this is the best way to provide recompense. If a country has a monopoly of literary talent it might seem sensible to nationalize that industry, employ the literary producers as any other employee, and claim ownership of the product – plays, poems, films, music or whatever – for the nation. But business interests are not always consistent, and some potential business projects might conflict directly with individual information rights. For example, in the USA in the 1980s large numbers of formerly government publications were hived off to private interests, which were given the freedom to determine not only the price of the product but also the format in which it appeared. So, big series were potentially to be made available only as computer files, and at whatever price the market would bear. This was a potential loss of access to government information for many, who might well have argued that they have paid through taxes for the publications already anyway.

At some time in the 1980s, when data protection legislation was being introduced, some business interests toyed (but did not go ahead with, because it was outlawed) with the idea of setting up 'data havens' where businesses could store data outside the provisions of data protection legislation. This seems to be a case where business activity would have been in direct conflict with individual information rights, but again it is not clear that all or even necessary business activity must be in conflict with information rights for individuals.

Currently there are some interesting cases where the future is not clear. Social networking software works on the basis of people making open declarations about themselves, declarations that might put them at risk of data or identity theft or fraud, but which serves as the basis for the business of selling the advertising space on the social networking sites. Superficially these sites aid interpersonal communication, so all parties benefit. Of course, information businesses have developed so successfully in the last few decades that access to their public services might now seem almost a necessity, so would it be reasonable to claim that access to the internet, or mobile phones, was a right?

Discussion of the interests of business are less likely to centre on areas of conflict with individual information rights than would be the case with governments, but we can note two special cases. First, where governments are requiring businesses to retain records of mobile phone calls and texts, and the businesses are complying. Integrity of your personal correspondence is a recognized right, and this might seem to put that at risk. Similarly, government plans to maintain DNA databases for whole populations (an action under consideration by the British government) will require the technical assistance of IT firms, who will be happy to have the business. Some governments also interfere with e-mail communication and with internet access. Where access is denied it is not quite the same as interfering with mail, but the two are related.

Common good

Finally, can any notion of 'common good' supersede claims for individual information rights? Common good arguments are usually introduced in individual circumstances even though their appeal is to an overall benefit. It is not clear that common good arguments are mutually compatible. Usually common good arguments are used to circumscribe or curtail rights but not to supplant or suppress them. For example, freedom of speech might be limited so that we do not allow incitement of racial or religious hatred, but that still allows freedom of most speech. If you discovered the cure to an illness that afflicted millions worldwide, AIDS, for example, or arthritis, then it might be for the common good that you were denied the intellectual property rights that would allow your enrichment in favour of offering a cheap cure to millions, but that would not supplant general intellectual property rights. 'Common good' should not be confused with 'goods in common', where scarce resources are shared by a community to mutual benefit, or to the benefit of each in turn. In this case the rights are ascribed rights that subtend from the sharing arrangement.

We could argue, in the three cases of government and business interests and the common good, that individual information rights might fairly be curtailed but not abolished, and so even if we allow the primacy of any of these alternative claims there will still be room for some level of individual information rights, but we would have moved away from arguing that the whole information policy should be based on information rights. In fact, no one has argued that case, and it can be put forward only as a thought experiment to see what might happen if it were tried. We might start from the principle that information rights should be observed, but we might find practical difficulties in implementing such a principle.

If we take the counter position that in principle the interests of government, business or the common good must always be presumed to take precedence in determining information policy we face a strong assault on the case for information rights, but we are also left with residual cases where the three alternative interests have no claim and so there will still be some aspects of information policy that could be met by information rights. For example, freedom of information may be an annoyance for governments that could be dispensed with, and data protection similarly a burden for central administration to ensure and so could also be abandoned, but freedom of expression, although an annoyance at times, and potentially a threat to civil order, embodies a principle that we give testimony, speak the truth, as for example in legal cases. It would be difficult to maintain that we are allowed to speak the truth in court but that in the street outside there is no protection for such speech. We need to build the habit and the acceptance of normality for speaking the truth. Civil society depends on an expectation that people will speak the truth. Some level of right of freedom of expression is understood, and not easily dispensed with. In some form information rights will remain.

The claim that there are no rights, and the other claim that rights are a luxury that we can only intermittently afford, are easily dealt with. Information rights, although they embody principles, are not argued for as natural rights. They tend to be understood as rights that are ascribed, usually by law but otherwise by general social acceptance. It may be, for example, that we maintain that there is a right to privacy, even though there is no law of privacy or that such a law proves impossible to enforce: we think that the idea of privacy is inviolate and should be given effect. When British parliamentarians were publicly shown to be making excessive expenses claims we accepted that their privacy was being invaded, but felt that the disclosure was in the public interest and thus their privacy claims could be ignored. Ascribing rights means they exist as political, social or civil rights but do not have strong claims as moral or universal rights. Even so, we have included for the last 60 years as standard elements in statements and treaties about rights a number of information rights. Before turning to these rights, and how they give us a basis for information policy, we will look briefly at the list of information rights generated by Ann Wells Branscomb (1985).

Ann Wells Branscomb's information rights

Ann Wells Branscomb's information rights are:

1 to know information about ourselves and the world we live in
2 to collect information – investigative function
3 to acquire information archived by others
4 to withhold information about ourselves – personal, corporate, national
5 to control the release of information
6 to receive compensation for information (profit)
7 to protect information – security
8 to destroy or expunge information
9 to correct or alter information
10 to publish or disseminate information – access to the marketplace.

This list gives us a working base for calculating what an information policy might contain if it were based on information rights for individuals. There are two benefits from using this strategy. One, we can understand directly the impact of these rights by thinking of how they would affect us personally. Second, they give us a programme for setting policy in a wide range of areas, some of which are not directly information related.

The right to have information about the world we live in, sometimes reified in rights documents as the right to receive information, is a natural requirement for us to understand ourselves as individuals. But what does that mean? Does it mean we have a right to know about the conditions of our environment, whether we are being exposed to hazardous chemicals? Does it mean we have a right to learn about our bodies, the developmental changes we will go through, and what will happen to us when we die? Although it specifies a right to know, does it also mean a right to change these things? Does an information right carry with it the right to act? Does it mean that adopted children have the right to know who their natural parents are? Does this right exist for all persons, including prisoners, psychiatric patients, children and enlisted soldiers? Most people would answer affirmatively to most of these questions, but what if the information would disturb people – information about environmental hazards, for example? If you have a right to some information and you get that information, are you obliged to act on it, or will you lose later if you make a claim over some issue that was publicized long ago? Actually, most of these points are of no concern: information policy is a policy, the consequences are a different question.

Branscomb's second right, the right to seek out information, to investigate, is also a crucial right. Without it, no science could take place, no journalists could operate, and we would all be limited to the information that others decided should be made available to us. The third right, to acquire information archived by others, is also important. It is the basis for shared knowledge, and a precondition for the transfer of information through time and across generations.

The fourth right, the right to withhold information about yourself – whether it be your person, your company or your nation, is also a critical basis for many standard elements of information policy but it may seem to be in conflict with the previous right. Withholding information about the nation is the basis for agreed measures to protect state secrets. This is not controversial, although the point at which information is deemed to be secret may be controversial – as evidenced by the long-term discussions over the British Official Secrets Act alluded to above. The list of accepted exceptions to an open regime about official information is well known and well agreed, but there are areas of discretion that spark debate. The recent move to introduce freedom of information policies shows that there was a recognized need to relax levels of state secrecy; the continuing debate about freedom of information shows that the tensions between state interests and the idea of open government continue to fuel discussion. Companies, like states, need to protect information about themselves, and, like states, companies seek information on their competitors. Politely, this is called gathering market intelligence; less politely, it is spying – to discover a competitor's financial situation, new research plans, marketing strategies or even the personal habits of employees. Companies need to protect this information about themselves as part of their strategy to stay in business – and simultaneously they will be seeking the same information about others. The question that arises here is not should they be able to protect themselves, but what level of protection is permitted? For example, a drinks manufacturer may want to keep the ingredients of a product secret, to protect its product from copying, but public health officials may want the ingredients publicly disclosed.

Personal information is slightly different. You may just want to keep certain details about yourself private. You may not want to discuss publicly your health or financial problems, or who you go on holiday with, or even where you buy your food. Your reasons for this may just be that you want to keep this information to yourself, not because you are at risk in any way if it is revealed. Other information, where you are doing something out of the ordinary, you may want to keep private for other reasons – if you are applying for a job you may wish to conceal this from your current employer or colleagues. The point is that we don't have to justify things about ourselves – unless there are good reasons for others to know. If you have an infectious disease others may feel that they should have this information to protect their own interests. At what point is the border crossed? It may be crossed at different points with people in the public eye, compared with average citizens.

It is not possible to make these rights absolute, for countries, companies or individuals. If a state starts manufacturing nuclear weapons there is usually an international outcry; if a company starts dumping toxic waste we think it should be investigated, and if you have typhoid I want to know.

Branscomb's fifth right, to control the release of information, relates to the fourth. We decide when we tell people that we are to get married, or that we are changing jobs, or we decide not to tell anyone that we have won the lottery. This is an element of privacy. Building this into information policy is more difficult. For example, newspapers thrive on releasing information before anyone else, as do all journalists, so if we prohibit them from releasing information about people, how could they do their business – a business which we seem to accept as legitimate? In this case, and in others, there is no set of algorithms that we can apply to determine when the policy provisions about privacy can be set aside. Policy has to be as effective as law, less rigid, but applied with certainty. We cannot make provisions that say it is forbidden to release information about persons without their consent except by a journalist. Quite independently, there is the question of who is a journalist. If you are caught up in some international event and start phoning in the news to a TV station as the events unfold, are you going to be told that your story is unacceptable because you are not a certified journalist? The employee who revealed the details of British parliamentarians' expenses was not a journalist. Providing for exceptions is difficult, but effective information policy demands it.

Branscomb's sixth right, the right to receive compensation, to make a profit, is interesting, very acceptable, but also controversial. If you take photographs of two famous people closeted together and then sell these photographs to the highest bidder you would be availing yourself of this right, but the public might think your practice unacceptable. The photographs would clearly be yours – whether you took them yourself, hired someone to take them, or bought them from the original photographer. However, there have been times when the public interest has been well served by such photographs, particularly when political, commercial or illegal activities are involved. But mostly we think this would be invasion of privacy. However, the right to sell a book, a film script or a piece of music you have written is recognized and accepted. Branscomb's right is one we mostly want to accept, probably cannot manage without, but still we see there may be exceptions. The world needs protection for the right to sell ideas and expressions of ideas.

The seventh right, to protect information, to keep it secure, is also very important. This is a right that mostly we demand of other people. When we sacrifice information, especially private information, about ourselves, we have a right to expect that the recipient will not be careless of that information, will not use it for profit independently of the reason we surrendered it, and will ensure that the information does not fall into the wrong hands. This is the right of data protection, and, unlike privacy, legislatures have largely put in place some level of protection for data and also require that data will not be exported to environments that offer a lower level of protection. There are two elements to this right: the right to have data kept physically secure, and not be made public, and the right that no unauthorized use will be made of the data by those who have legitimate access to it.

The eighth right, the right to destroy or expunge information, is associated with the previous right. Between the two we can see a requirement that information about us is accurate, and that any records are kept up to date and are corrected if they are wrong. That issue is covered by Branscomb's ninth point. With the eighth right we can require people who no longer need information about us to destroy what they have. We can also expect certain types of record to be expunged when they have run their course. Finally, Branscomb cites as the tenth right the right to publish or to disseminate information – the right to have access to the marketplace. This right can also be seen as a right to participate in public debate, or at least to make known your views about current issues, or indeed anything. So, under Branscomb's argument you could claim a right to leaflet your neighbourhood, or the whole country, about missing pets, unsuitable political leaders, financial wrong-doing, or unacceptable national policies, like an unjust war, or merely make announcements about a garage sale or the significance of an imminent solar eclipse. Her case also allows you to make money from these activities if you can.

The overall impression we get from Branscomb's list is that rights central to maintaining the person's integrity are particularly important, but that anyone also has rights that extend out into the community. What we do not find listed are those 'negative' rights that make access to information possible, the first level rights, and those second level rights like education and literacy that make it possible to make use of information. Perhaps we should also have an explicit right to have our rights protected and our ability to enjoy them assured. Do all these amount to an information policy?

The answer must be 'No', because, although they do protect individuals and their information interests, they say too little about reconciling conflicts of rights between people, or between people and communities, and they say nothing about how to manage the relationship between the information interests of collectivities – companies, churches, voluntary associations, even families, and local communities and nation states – and individuals. They also say nothing about reconciling conflicts of information rights interests between any of these collectivities. Branscomb's list of rights remains interesting, however, because from it we learn how to balance the claims put forward previously about information societies or public spheres, or on behalf of government interests or business interests, with those of individuals.

We can say that a set of policies built around Branscomb's claims would represent a strong theory of information policy because they would be designed explicitly to bring about the realization of the rights listed. They could also have some degree of autonomy, because where the implications of the provisions mentioned by Branscomb are not fully worked out, in terms of how they handle conflicts of rights or how they create power bases for collective groups, the policies could have effects well beyond Branscomb's intentions. For example, provisions about information security, which currently seem to be either lax or weakly applied in several countries, may create power for people who have to determine who may have access to which information. There are other areas of policy, freedom of information, for example, that Branscomb's provisions scarcely cover, except by inference (the right to know about our world, the right to seek information), which would have to exist in some form, so information policy in total would have an autonomy beyond Branscomb. The case of censorship, or at least its control, extends these points.

Internationally recognized rights

That we have to legislate for information policy shows that people and governments do not naturally behave in a way that ensures our information rights are protected. That international treaties have identified several information rights among human rights in general shows that there are serious claims that information rights extend beyond political or civil rights to be included among natural or moral rights.

What are these internationally recognized rights, and how well maintained are they? In recent years both the British and the Irish governments have introduced legislation incorporating the European Convention on Human Rights into national law, suggesting that previous legal provisions did not offer a satisfactory level of protection for such rights. On the other hand, there have been objections to this incorporation of human rights provisions into these legal systems, with claims that obsessive adherence to human rights provisions is interfering with the fight against terrorism. This counter claim might suggest that some human rights protections are now seen by some people as too generous. It is not clear that any information rights are considered controversial.

The Universal Declaration of Human Rights 1948

What is clear is that all rights identified in the Universal Declaration of Human Rights (UDHR) are identified literally as universal; they apply to anyone, so there is no restriction against people in prison or any other category of person, and the rights apply 'without distinction of any kind, such as race, colour, sex, language, religion, political or other opinion, national or social origin, property, birth or other status' (Article 2). The preamble makes clear that inalienable rights are the foundation of freedom, justice and peace, and that freedom of speech (*inter alia*) is the 'highest aspiration of the common people'. More interestingly, the declaration preamble also makes clear that the declaration is to promote 'the development of friendly relations between nations' and 'social progress and better standards of life in larger freedom'.

So, despite the initial appearance that the rights enumerated in the UDHR are absolute rights in themselves, we have to understand them as means towards an end, indeed an end connected with social progress and relations between nation states, and so closely connected to some overall vision of what society might be like. This is emphasized by Article 29, which states that everyone has duties to their community 'in which alone the free and full development of his personality is possible', and that 'In the exercise of his rights and freedoms, everyone shall be subject only to such limitations as are determined by law solely for the purpose of securing due recognition and respect for the rights and freedoms of others and of meeting the just requirements of morality, public order and the general welfare in a democratic society.'

Rights are subordinate to community and society, and the individual needs a community to realize his potential. Individual rights seem to lose potency as a basis for formation of information policy when we have the UDHR and subsequent declarations of human rights in mind.

However, we still do have the enumerated information rights, and they are worth emphasizing, especially as freedom of speech was mentioned specifically. The best known is Article 19, but articles 12, 17, 18, 20, and 26 and 27 are also worth our attention. To start we can discuss some of the implications of Article 21, which declares the right of everyone to take part in the government of their country, either directly or indirectly through representatives. At the minimum this can be seen as a right to vote periodically, but we can also infer other entailments from this. Freedom of information, the right to get information, particularly documents, about government activity, is not expressly mentioned in the

UDHR. Legislation for freedom of information typically came 20 to 40 years later than the Declaration, but in this Article 21 we can see the basis for freedom of information. In the UDHR rights are enumerated but the means for their realization are not. So, the capacity people need to enjoy their rights are implied – because if you don't have the capacity you can't enjoy the right. Moreover, you must also have the capability – you must have the necessary level of education and skill, and the need for this is recognized in article 26.

Intellectual property rights are more expressly recognized, both in Article 17, which recognizes the right to own property, and in Article 27, which itemizes intellectual property rights: 'Everyone has the right to the protection of the moral and material interests resulting from any scientific, literary or artistic production of which he is the author.' And again, following the last discussion, the need for capacity and capability means that legislation must be put in place to protect intellectual property. This, we can interpret, means that information policy issues are very strong. The information rights identified in the UDHR must be seen as autonomous, and they also constitute a strong theory of information policy, because they must exist if we allow that rights exist.

However, there are caveats to add to this. Those rights relating to privacy and the integrity of the individual (articles 12, 18 and 22) are uncontroversial, but Article 19 has an interesting history. This article, cited as the right that guarantees freedom of expression and therefore denies censorship, the right 'to seek, receive and impart information and ideas through any media and regardless of frontiers', has obviously not always been upheld, and people claiming its protection have also been under severe threat to their lives. More importantly for this discussion is the failure to keep the word 'seek' in subsequent declarations, conventions, covenants and treaties. The 1966 International Covenant of Human Rights added 'national security' to the grounds for restricting rights to information, and Article 20 itemized the media in which ideas and opinions could be expressed – thereby limiting to those media the possible outlets for freedom of expression.

More glaringly, the earlier (1950) European Convention on Human Rights (which has been adopted into British and also Irish law) excluded the right to seek information, and also limited rights of access to information. The Helsinki agreement (CSCE) gave only vague statements about information rights. This was partly corrected in the subsequent Copenhagen agreement (1991) but the right to seek information was limited to information about human rights – a rather severe restriction. Recently 'seek' has come back into international rights documents, and it obviously is of major importance, as without it no scientific or journalistic endeavour would be permitted. Once again, despite this recovery, we must recall the restrictions permitted by Article 29 of the UDHR, which can allow the complete withdrawal of rights.

Overall, the situation about Information rights is ambivalent. Although itemized, incorporated into law and with international courts to give judgements, they are not secure. But, they provide an interesting basis for the formation of information policies, and it is possible to argue both for and against the idea of rights as a foundation for information policy. We now should turn away from these overarching social context arguments about information policies and look at the way individual sectors can be legislated for.

Part 2
Information policy sectors

THE DISCUSSION IN preceding chapters about the operating context for information policies shows that much depends on how you see that context, both for an understanding of what information policies can do and for generating ideas about what they might do. The final examination of human rights in information also showed that where law brings them into existence information policies, both generally and in particular sectors, do exist and we must recognize them. Even if a country has no law about, say, intellectual property ownership, there is still that set of human rights principles that can be appealed to as an argument that morally and inherently such rights do exist and this can act as a spur to those who want to campaign for legislation. The focus on what exists, in the moral imagination or in enforceable laws, brings us back to consider what happens in particular sectors, and the debate about the effects of the current state of law and custom and its enforcement and how things should change, or can proceed.

In the following chapters we will look at four areas of activity: censorship and freedom of expression, privacy and data protection, freedom of information, and intellectual property. This is not an exhaustive list but it will serve us with examples that cover the points that need to be made about strategies and policy development. In examining individual sectors we will not be looking for comprehensive statements of the current state of law or practice; these are well covered in other excellent works that relate to particular jurisdictions.

The points that need to be uncovered here are those that indicate the range of possibilities, the history of practice, and the basis for arguments about what could or should be done. Knowing what an information policy should look like, what it should cover and contain, depends in part on understanding the operating context and the theoretical underpinnings that we have already considered, but it also depends on knowing the range of what is possible and what effects various policy instruments will have on daily life. When we look at the way policies and laws and customs play out 'on the street' we must see them in a context where people think not of the rightness or otherwise of some particular law or practice but more of general concepts like justice and truth and their sense of personal identity and integrity, and also of how in a self-interested way it will affect them. Seen that way laws on censorship, or whatever, must take account of the 'facts of life' and the forms of life people have. Such concerns for forms of life must be general, for in any jurisdiction one law must apply to all people, but also they must be workable. If law or policy in any area does not work effectively the principle it supposedly recognizes is eroded and devalued. So, if there is no mechanism to offer people redress for theft of their intellectual property, then the idea of intellectual property protection is weakened.

The first question we shall examine is censorship, which we will consider alongside freedom of expression. These topics will be explored in some depth, to show how a case for freedom of expression can be built up. Subsequently the three other topics will be discussed in the light of what the examination of censorship and freedom of expression shows us.

5

Censorship, freedom of speech and freedom of expression

FIRST, **WE NEED** to explore the relationship between these terms, which are slightly different but intricately related. The topic that most excites comment and draws criticism is censorship, which overwhelmingly people instinctively think of as wrong. Yet, when asked about what we should allow children to view or read, at the least we think we should provide guidance for them and if that is not possible we quickly arrive at a point where, we think for the best, some things are concealed from children. Typically, we conceal harmful or illegal content, and the European Union (EU) has a directive for member states to protect minors against such material by restricting it as they think best. Censorship is a cry that is raised in other circumstances, too. We are reluctant to broadcast material on bomb-making, particularly nuclear weapons, biological agents that might incapacitate, injure or kill, or material that might be mentally disturbing for some categories of patients in secure hospitals. The list is easily extended; the question is, where does it stop?

It is clear that we want to limit the range of material that can automatically be banned, and also limit the classes of people who can be denied access to any material they want to see. If we don't agree to such a limitation we are handing over to those with power and coercive authority – usually but not exclusively governments – the freedom to deny access at will as suits them, and without any certainty that the ban

will be removed when any temporary need is over. This is just a matter of experience, and that fact brings us closer to the real world where
we must consider what actually happens as well as what we intend. If
you ban a child from going to the cinema to see certain types of film
you may find that you have, apparently, got a compliant child, but it
may later turn out that when the child visits friends they watch even
worse material downloaded or on videos: policy decisions and the strategies used to implement them do not always lead to the intended results.

Censorship, when effective, stops the production and distribution of
certain material; how that can happen we will consider next, but first
we should note some differences between freedom of speech and freedom of expression. Freedom of speech is a loose term that describes the
situation that we believe we have in western democracies, where, by and
large, people can say what they like, within certain well known limits.
In some places these limits are removed. For example in the UK parliament 'parliamentary privilege' allows MPs speaking in the chamber of
the House of Commons in the course of parliamentary business (note
the limitations) to make allegations against named people that would
be illegal or at least leave the MP open to legal action if spoken outside.
Similarly, there is a spot on the corner of a central London park called
Speakers' Corner, where anyone may make any speech they like. This
facility does not offer the protection that parliamentary privilege offers,
but usually wild statements made there are tolerated as long as the facility is not abused. Freedom to speak is guaranteed under the Universal
Declaration of Human Rights and is an essential prerequisite for any
working democratic system of government.

'To speak' here is a broad term, covering written work, cartoons,
visual and maybe other types of material. Usually these are collected
together under the term 'utterances'. There are other actions that may
convey a message or signal a position that the term 'utterance' may not
cover. If you decide to walk together with other people in a public place
at a previously publicly announced time in connection with some issue
or event you may be a peaceful demonstrator, or you might be commit-

ting a public order offence if you are challenging other actions. This book began with the example of the demonstrations in London in 2009 against the meeting of the G20 group of world leaders, and referred to various records of the event that surfaced in various media. Demonstrators everywhere are making a statement, even if they say no words: their association with the publicity for the event, march or demonstration speaks for them. By joining the march they exercize their right to associate freely with others to make their point.

This is freedom of expression, perhaps slightly wider than freedom of speech. You do not need to be marching with others or in association with others to make some expression about an issue. If you climb Big Ben in London, tie yourself to the railings of the White House, or stand in front of an army tank in Tiananmen Square you are expressing yourself. You could be protesting about the plight of the whales, the lack of rights for fathers, or for some person or group of people you feel sympathy for, and you may have some placard or banner or you could be making a speech. The point is that you are doing something unusual for that particular place: tying yourself to the railings outside your own home might be useful if you are in the midst of some domestic dispute, or a dispute with your neighbours, but not much use otherwise. The expression usually connects a place that is significant for the protest you wish to make with some action that draws attention to yourself. We tolerate this, but sometimes the actions get to the point where authorities want to invoke laws that allow them to disperse a protest march because it threatens public order, blocks normal routeways, or is a danger to public health. Your right to express yourself is an important information right, even if the form of expression communicates only a very general message – that you are protesting against some action.

What we are encountering here is a form of utterance that authorities sometimes want to suppress for reasons other than, or in addition to, the content. If you protest against nuclear weapons by joining a march, a government committed to keeping nuclear weapons may not like the expression of dissent, but it may also find the form that dissent

takes is independent of content and uses inconvenience or embarrass-
ment to others to make its point. A march could take place for any number of reasons: we cannot say of any group of marching protesters that
there is one particular message that is being communicated; this week's
march could be about an entirely different issue from last week's. So,
censorship sometimes attempts to muzzle speech or expression by intercepting content, and sometimes by intercepting the form of the expression in a content-neutral way. The interception might be associated with
place but also with time. If you write a letter to a newspaper protesting
against some government action, that is content specific. If you have a
loud and heated dispute in a residential street at 3 a.m. and the neighbours object, their objection is (most likely) content neutral.

Various authorities have power to intercept or control speech acts and
expressions of concern. Commonly they are the various arms of government, but they might in some societies include churches or religious bodies – and historically in Europe most notoriously churches exercised
coercive powers to control speech and publication, and individuals also
have power through the courts to seek redress for any speech that
defames them or interferes with their rights. Furthermore, governments
or their various subordinate agencies have the power to influence (as
opposed to control) speech, or to set the conditions in which speech or
expression can get publicity. This includes ways to control the frame of
mind of the population, so that although your speech is not suppressed,
it might be ignored by those it is aimed at, because they have been educated to discount it. A pacifist in wartime would have trouble convincing a population that was committed to the conflict and emotionally or
psychologically engaged in it to cease the struggle and seek peace. So,
what are these means of influence, and what other powers are available
to authorities to intercept messages? And how do we determine what
is the legitimate extent of government power in respect of controlling
communications?

Powers of intervention

Governments can intervene in information markets in various ways. We can easily identify six:

- by investigating the market
- by regulating the market
- by competing in the market
- by arbitrating in the market
- by creating monopolies
- by legislating over content.

Investigating the market can operate in several ways. First, the act of investigation can lead to the deferment of any action, and induce caution in those who might fear that their speech or information products might become the subject of investigation. For example, every so often there is concern in Britain about apparent outrageous intrusions into the private lives of various people. In the worst case, when the available mechanisms seem to fail (the Press Complaints Commission never seems to be able to control this matter), a commission of inquiry might be set up under government auspices to investigate the possibility of a law on privacy. While such commissions are in progress the incidence of invasions of privacy seem to abate. Inquiries into the distribution of scarce or limited resources (for example the distribution of space on the broadcast spectrum) can also condition behaviour of interested parties.

Following investigation, or independently, markets can be regulated. Many industries that are either fully or partly funded by taxpayers, but which are not under direct government control, are subject to regulatory bodies. Other industries that have no public funding element can also be subject to state regulation. So, broadcasting industries, which often include both publicly funded and commercial organizations, may be subject, as in Britain, to the regulator. Regulation can include rules about content, programme mix, wavelengths, hours of broadcasting, programme sourcing and maybe other issues like language mix. Other information exchange activities may also be subject to more direct regulation either as after-the-fact intervention, like the information commissioner, or before-the-fact stipulation, again like the information commissioner. The framework of regulation may be centrally determined within the structure of existing government departments, or a matter of general legislation, or as a consequence of international treaties and their institutions (for example the World Trade Organization) but in all cases it gives governments power over what can be transmitted, generated, distributed or viewed in a general sense – regulating types of content rather than actual content.

Governments can also compete in markets, either by developing commercial organizations of their own or by according other operators favourable status. It is said that the former Soviet Embassy in London had a daily order for 25,000 copies of one British newspaper that the Soviet authorities supported, thereby giving the newspaper the commercial basis for its operations. In some cases the government competition is not an interference in the market. Governments publishing their own publications are not competing with other publishers, but they may, if they keep prices below cost recovery levels, effectively keep other alternative publishers out of that part of the market.

Governments can also arbitrate in markets where there are disputes or where current commercial operators need encouragement to co-operate or amalgamate to create a smaller number of commercially viable units. This way of influencing markets and what is produced for them is most obvious in the judicial function, where laws are set to determine the framework of activities of operators and the courts are used to enforce that framework. This can be the operation of either private law to protect individual interests or public law to restrain operators from publishing, for example, harmful or illegal content.

One case that is proving difficult to regulate or arbitrate is the internet, although various countries constrain internet service providers to ensure control over content and access. Were it the case that all internet access was via cable it would not be difficult to control access or content, but as signals are distributed via satellite the footprint may not correspond with national frontiers and so it could prove difficult to restrict content or access, even where the courts have formal power, because of a lack of jurisdiction. Some interesting examples have included the sale of Nazi memorabilia over e-Bay, which was accessible in Germany. Nazi memorabilia is illegal in Germany and the German authorities sought ways to stop access to e-Bay sales of such material. Currently European directives leave it to national parliaments and governments to regulate content. Sometimes government attempts to use the courts to interfere with information markets fail. In the late 1980s the British government sought to stop the sale of the memoirs of a former secret agent, who had signed an agreement (and also the Official Secrets Act) not to publish material relating to his work. The British government spent huge sums of money seeking to restrain publication in the UK, Australia and other places. As the book was freely on sale in Dublin the government efforts were in vain.

Finally, the government can create monopolies, either by taking over all existing operators and combining them into one state-owned utility, or by handing out franchises which may be territorial or subject related. The former covers the case of all the major European nations' post and telephone companies. For a generation the EU has been trying to break up these monopolies, but even where alternative operators are permitted to offer services it is the case in Britain, Ireland and France that the national operator still has a monopoly of supplying the first telephone line to subscribers. Governments have also created franchises, which are auctioned from time to time for regional television and radio services. The sixth way, legislating over content, what we normally call laws of censorship, is the subject of the next chapter.

These six ways of influencing markets, which mostly but not always do not interfere with individual instances of content or access, still have a major effect on the degree of freedom to make and distribute utterances. Governments also have very powerful arbitrary powers over the way information market players can operate. For example, requirements that mobile phone operators store records of mobile phone conversations and texts, as part of a range of efforts to counter the threat of terrorism and other organized crime, is not a requirement that the phone operators can refuse, but it has major implications for the nature of the state and its relations with its citizens.

Governments also have economic sanctions available to them that can affect the operations of the information market and the capacity of citizens to disseminate their views. Some of these we have already discussed – like creating monopolies – but others should also be mentioned, even though in most cases we have not experienced them in recent years. First, governments can control access to materials, such as paper and ink. During World War 2 newsprint in Britain was rationed and publishers had to show that their intended publication would contribute to the war effort. Modern equivalents include controlling access to the information technology needed to access the internet, controlling access to the necessary knowledge to use the technology, and controlling access to telephone calls. Governments can also control economic aspects of the information business by imposing taxes and levies. Perhaps the most notorious tax was the stamp duty payable on all periodical publications up to the 1850s in the UK and Ireland. The tax was so high that, effectively, poorer people could not afford to buy newspapers: it was an effective way of controlling access to information and the eventual removal of the duty heralded the age of the free press.

Governments can also create monopolies, as discussed above, and they can deal with interested or powerful parties to create private monopolies by assisting in the process of take-overs, by making entry into an industry difficult for further operators, or by the award of government contracts that guarantee levels of business. More interestingly, governments can control access to necessary technologies by creating monopolies, by regulating the supply of or denying access to necessary raw materials, or by regulating access to skilled personnel. One current area of interest is the attempts of the French government to protect its film industry against the importation of cheap Hollywood programmes and films. This process of subsidies has been mentioned above. We should also mention the power of governments or legislators to vary levels of economic reward, such as the level of copyright or patent protection. A small level of protection for inventors and authors will discourage further work by them, as will the lack of an enforcement mechanism. Protection for inventors that is too restrictive of trade will act against the dissemination of ideas, so a balance has to be struck.

An interesting current example is the introduction, in some countries, under EU pressure, of a *droit de suite*, whereby artists are entitled to a share of any future sale of their work – their financial interest is not exhausted at the point of initial sale, and through subsequent sales they may be able to offer some prospect of financial reward and support for their families. It has been alleged that this will act as a restraint on trade, and that works of art will be sold in New York, where such a right does not exist, rather than in the original European country, just to avoid the extra costs which the new right will entail. Governments, by their attitude to this issue, can indicate support for artists or display their desire to protect the market. One further restraint on trade exists in Britain whereby important works of art that are sold to overseas buyers may be kept in the country if enough money can be raised to recompense the vendor for the lost sale. This does not affect content, although it does have some impact on access.

Finally, we should note the range of penalties that governments can impose, which effectively gives them the coercive power that forces us to consider all the issues raised above when we consider how, at a practical level, utterances and expressions can be disseminated, or that dissemination can be arrested.

Penalties have included fines, imprisonment, execution and mutilation, loss of economic privileges and powers, and confiscation of products, production machinery, other equipment and materials. If you decide to go into the information business by setting up your own printing press to produce likenesses of paper money – pound notes, dollar bills or whatever, it is most likely that you will be arrested, fined and imprisoned, that your production equipment and materials will be confiscated and your product, the counterfeit paper money, will be burnt. If you break other legislation – for example in the UK there are strict controls on what may be reported in criminal law cases before the courts, and if you publish material in contravention of that you will be charged with contempt of court and will have to purge that contempt by making a statement in court – you will probably be fined and may be imprisoned until you have paid the fine. This, we should note, is really about protecting the legal process and ensuring there is no interference with it and that no undue influence is used to influence witnesses or jurors, but it just happens to be about the distribution of information.

In other jurisdictions, like the USA, different rules about court reporting apply. If you persistently breach the conditions of a licence to broadcast radio or TV programmes you will probably lose the licence and you will lose the economic power that the licence gave. Execution and mutilation of information industry workers has not occurred in the UK or Ireland for centuries, although we should note that William Cobbett was in danger of prosecution in the early 19th century for evading the Stamp Acts. In the 16th century John Prynne was mutilated (his ears were cut off) for publishing material contrary to government wishes. However, in our current era journalists have been executed by non-government groups in various countries in North Africa and the Middle East. Each year journalists are imprisoned. Twenty years ago the translator and publisher of a translation of Salman Rushdie's *Satanic Verses* were killed, and Rushdie was forced into hiding. In his case independent operators were attempting to carry out the wishes of senior figures in the Iranian state and government structure. During the Watergate crisis, at a time when the reporters on the story still lacked corroborating evidence, the *Washington Post* feared for its economic survival, not because of direct government pressure (although that was forthcoming) but because of the threat to the finances of the paper if legal action was taken against it. These latter cases are not instances of direct penalty or punishment after due process or even after administrative intervention (as could be the case with actions of a data protection or privacy commissioner), but indicate more insidious influences attempting to frighten off critics by threats.

Other forms of censorship

We should note that quite apart from direct laws about censorship, there is a wide variety of other agencies and instruments that can interfere, disrupt, stop or change any 'utterances' before they reach any readers or viewers. We are familiar with censorship boards in some countries, but there is a wide variety of practice. For printed products most censorship boards ban rather than censor, though in some countries journals are censored by overprinting parts of the text, or maybe advertisements, with thick printer's ink. Printed products are usually either permitted, with or without the text intact, or they are banned; they are not usually graded, as happens with films and videos.

In the UK there is no censorship of publications board, instead the police act to seize materials and promote prosecutions when they believe the Obscene Publications Act has been breached, yet films are still graded by a film censorship board. The use of an act supposedly removes subjective judgements and entrusts the decision to the court and the jury, but the mechanism is cumbersome. In the USA there is no procedure to censor printed materials, but other techniques have been used. The Comstock Acts prohibited the transmission of obscene material through the mails, and 24 states adopted similar legislation. When an exhibition of homo-erotic photographs by Robert Mapplethorpe was touring art galleries and exhibition centres the government acted to ensure that, although they could not censor or ban the exhibition, no public money would be used to support the exhibition, so in effect the exhibition was excluded from all publicly funded exhibition spaces.

In Ireland the Censorship of Publications Board has acquired fame for its very active policy in the period from its inception in 1929 until 1967, during which time a wide range of materials, including many that are regarded as part of the canon of 20th-century Irish literature, were banned. More recently the Board has allowed the magazine *Playboy* to be distributed, but banned a book of photographs that very graphically depicted human corpses after road accidents. The Irish board has also received requests to ban various works about witches, although they have not acted on these requests.

Sometimes authority to prosecute is delegated. In the USA in the 19th century the Comstock Acts allowed individual prosecutions by Comstock, who was made a special agent of the US Post Office for the purpose of enforcing the 1873 act, which he had promoted. In earlier times the religious authorities also had powers to ban or confiscate material, and in England from 1557 to 1640 the Stationers' Company entered into a mutually supportive agreement with the government whereby only books published by members of the Stationers' Company (apart from some religious authorities) were licenced, but in return the Stationers' Company made available for inspection all the works of its members, effectively acting as a conduit for government censorship while securing the monopoly for the company. There is also the possibility in most common law systems for private prosecutions for a tort or libel. Such actions rarely reach court as earlier agreements prior to publication avoid costly legal action but can effectively censor the text. Actions for contempt of court have already been mentioned.

There are also provisions through national legislation or international treaty (which is given effect through legislation) for administrative censorship, whereby agencies are given powers to intercept materials under the specific authority of an act and without need to seek court approval. Post offices through the International Postal Union are instructed to intercept harmful materials in the mail. This can include explosives and toxic materials, but also publications such as films, videos, magazines and books. Similarly the International Telecommunications Union bans the transmission of certain types of message – for example, abusive phone calls. Another agency with power to intercept goods is HM Revenue & Customs. This can, for example, hold goods, including publications, at the port of entry. Finally, there are acts that prohibit hate speech.

All these matters, the formal instruments for censorship, the coercive powers and penalties, and the various means of influencing readers and publishers are all part of the 'facts of life' that we must deal with in the real world. There are other aspects of the 'facts of life' that relate to the way individual people will act. They all constitute part of what we must take account of when determining how and what we should censor. The 'high level' understanding about what information policy is for, or the part it plays in constructing an information society or the public sphere, must take account of how it actually works. When we determine what kind of regime we want for censorship, or any other part of information policy, we must be confident that the mechanisms and instruments will work to bring into effect the intentions we have.

The history of censoring

We are familiar with current concerns about pornography, or sex and violence in films and TV programmes, but these have not always been the focus of the censor's attention. Over the period for which we have clear records the main concern of the censor has varied from sedition to blasphemy, to obscene images and texts, to religious and political opinion. The focus might vary in different jurisdictions at one time. In the UK from about 1450, the inception of printing, until about 1850 blasphemy was one of the major concerns, sometimes the most important. From 1517 until about 1700 religious opinion was also something that concerned the censor, sometimes very closely connected with sedition (which, to distinguish it from political opinion, we can call proposals to overthrow or undermine the political structure of the state or government).

After the end of the period of religious wars in Europe – usually agreed to be 1713 – religious opinion is replaced by political opinion as a concern for the censor, as republican and then democratic political opinion and movements began to threaten the traditional regimes in the major countries. Was there no pornography to worry about in this period? There was, but woodcut based illustrations lacked the refinement of detail that we are familiar with today and the publications were expensive to produce, so the market was limited. The mass production of cheap publications with high quality illustrations did not start until the 1840s, after the introduction of photography and rapid printing machinery.

As religious opinion and blasphemy receded as concerns, the way was left for obscenity, indecency and pornography to become the major focus of the censor's attention. The moral concerns of the censors were not limited to lurid images. Other issues, like contraception and abortion – matters that might be called issues to do with styles of life – called the censor's attention. So, we must recognize the influence of development in technology along with changes in intellectual and political life, as factors that could change the focus of censorship. It may be that something comes along that is perceived to be a more critical matter for the censor than obscenity, although it would be difficult to predict what it might be. Blasphemy seemed a potential candidate to make a comeback in the 1990s, but the renewed interest in blasphemy did not translate into a campaign to censor religious publications – at least, not in western countries. The pressure from Islamic leaders that followed the publication of some Danish cartoons in 2008 should be seen as political pressure, not a call for censorship. How the Danish and other western media respond will be an indication of how cowed they are by the reaction: a number of influences can lead people, organizations and states to self-select a line of policy. In libraries, for example, the decision to purchase one book from limited resources rather than another is a statement of a preference, not an act of censorship. My belief that books make excellent presents, and my family's belief that they do not, are both expressions of preferences; there is no suggestion that my family is seeking to censor anything. So, censorship focuses on different issues at different times, and our concern should not be what is right or wrong about censorship but more about how it can be made to work and what role it has in an information policy.

Making arguments for free speech

The next task we face is to examine just how we might go about constructing statements about how and what we censor. We can use this discussion as a basis for making similar observations about other aspects of information policy, like data protection or freedom of information. Conveniently there is in the work of Joshua Cohen (1993) a very useful argument for determining what kinds of speech (or utterances) should be protected and what kind we can safely allow to be controlled or censored. We will go through Cohen's argument and examine both the substantial point he is making and also comment on the structure that he puts forward to present his case. Cohen has a functional point to make: he wants to put forward a case for free speech that will help promote the effective working of a democratic society, so he rests his claims not on any arguments about morals but rather on what would sustain a democratic community.

6

Arguments for protecting speech

I N OUR CONSTRUCTION of information policy we need to have an understanding of how broad explanations of social movements are to be accounted for – whether we want to believe them, accommodate the possibility of them, or ignore them – and we also need to understand how the policies will work in day to day life at 'street level'. In between these two are the instruments and mechanisms that are meant to give effect to the intentions we have. These mechanisms need a rationale, a set of arguments that form the basis for the formation of policy. These arguments seem to stand on their own, so when we have discussions about censorship, intellectual property or whatever, we tend to see the issue in terms of the arguments that can be brought to bear about that particular issue. The strength of these arguments will have an impact on the effectiveness of the policy or law that is put in place, and they must be seen in the broader context of information policy overall. Whatever social analysis we might have we should also recall that often information policy issues tend to be secondary issues – so the protest in London in early 2009 is seen as an issue about world economic government, capitalism or policing policy, but rarely as an information issue, even though the intention of the protesters was to convey a message.

In constructing the argument there are three elements to consider. As an aside, let us just explain what we mean by the term 'an argument'.

We will often say that someone is arguing for a particular point, and that is the sense in which we are using the term, not in the sense of a strongly expressed disagreement. An argument is a claim supported by a series of testable propositions, where evidence of some sort is connected by some framework of justification to the main claim. Complex arguments may have many stages in each of which the claim and subordinate claims must be tested. First, the argument must offer a convincing or acceptable explanation of the real world situation. Second, the analysis of process and the desired outcomes must also be convincing. Third, the claims about the structure of the argument must be acceptable. So, when looking at Cohen's analysis of freedom of speech we must find all three components meet our criteria. In part we are examining Cohen's claims for their suitability as a solution to the freedom of speech problem, but we are also looking at the structure of his argument to see if it is portable to other information policy problems.

Cohen's analysis of freedom of speech

Cohen (1993) begins by asking general questions about why we might want to prohibit certain types of speech – what we do when we censor. The standard answers are that we are seeking to improve levels of civility, to punish levels of ignorance, or to protect people from what is upsetting or harmful. Cohen accepts that these are possible reasons, but that they are not comprehensive or deep enough. He adds to the list, or really supplants the list of superficial reasons with another list that includes protecting people from psychological injury, protecting people from indirect injury that might arise from encouraging assaults on target groups, and avoiding damage to prospects of equality. Immediately we have to accept that protecting or prohibiting certain speech is not an absolute issue in itself but achieves some social programme or objective. So, do we think that if we are unwilling to accept his list of reasons for protecting speech that all his claims are invalidated? And do we accept that we could accept the structure that seeks to find reasons for protection, even if we don't accept his particular list of reasons? This illustrates the parallel investigation we must pursue: Cohen's claims, and the structure of his argument. Why should we bother with the structure of his arguments?

There are few well worked out sets of explanations for information policy issues and using Cohen as a starting point is the best option open to us. Let us return to his rejection of the 'superficial' reasons for protecting speech. We can ask why we would seek to avoid upsetting people. There are daily experiences of upsetting events and use of speech. The news or the weather forecast may be upsetting, the language on some TV programme may upset me, or some event in the street where I witness a parent being rough with a child or rude to me may upset me, so why should we not just accept that there are upsetting things and not worry about speech? It must be that the idea of prohibiting speech to avoid upsetting people is not really convincing, and the varied experience of different countries will reinforce that.

So, there must be a deeper reason and Cohen's claim that we are seeking to avoid psychological injury carries more weight. His claim that we prohibit certain speech because we feel that such speech might threaten prospects of equality requires us to accept that the speech regime that we seek to promote must have some social or civil objectives, and that seems a better grounded reason than the claim that we are just seeking to promote civility. Why would we seek to promote civility just for its own sake: would we not lose some of the power of language if we limited the possible range of expression to that which did not shock? But there is a point, which Cohen seems to accept, that we want to avoid social disturbance that might arise if we tolerate speech that targets certain vulnerable groups. So, the disparity in permitted speech between the Nazi authorities and the Jewish communities in the 1933–1945 period is an example of what we seek to avoid, partly because the expression of hate serves no communicative purpose when it has been said once. Repetition merely makes communication more difficult (because it interferes with the possibility of dialogue and discussion), and so the purpose of having free speech in a community is lost.

The starting position

Cohen sets up two positions that he wants to assail in his defence of free speech. Structurally this is instructive, because in doing so he effectively limits the discussion to his variation on the two starting positions. Note that he does not start by discussing the claims of what could or should be censored; instead he takes two competing accounts of our protectionist attitudes to speech that identify why it should be protected. These two are the minimalist and the maximalist positions. The minimalist maintains that speech is just speech, it has no costs, no one is hurt by it, and no speech need be prohibited. In fact, in this view, it is best that all speech be protected, because we cannot trust governments. The maximalist view, as represented by Cohen, concedes that there are costs to speech, but that the benefits of free speech outweigh any costs. These are both simplistic visions, exceeded only by the view that there is no such thing as free speech, and that every issue must be decided on informally.

Cohen's response is to say that there is another way. He proposes that 'certain features of human motivation' render speech vulnerable to under-protection, and thus we need a rigid protection for speech. He proposes too that the costs of speech can be met by more speech. If you say something I find offensive the solution is not to muzzle you but to open up discussion so you hear the reasons I am offended by the speech, and I get to hear more about the background to your point of view – thus exemplifying those aspects of civility in speech that we determined were superficial reasons for censoring speech, but in this account become a means of extending the possibilities of what might be said. Finally, and in support of these first two points, Cohen says that protecting speech also secures certain fundamental interests that are critical for our existence. These interests he calls expressive, deliberative and informational.

So, the structure that Cohen gives us offers, first, a split account of what the approach to the subject matter should be, and then a 'third way', which is supported by the claim that it serves more interests and is more sophisticated as an analysis of the situation than either of the first two starting positions. Thus, he gives himself room to build an argument that is not constrained by currently available accounts. Of course, the success of this approach depends on the next stage in the claims being convincing, and first he has to build a picture that accounts for some current approaches to protecting speech and also gives some criteria that Cohen's own account must observe. These are what he calls the 'stringent' protections.

First, there is the presumption against content regulation. Earlier we discussed the difference between content neutral and content specific restrictions; now we must add a third category: viewpoint. If we ban speech in the street at 3 a.m., that is content neutral. If we ban the recommendation of some product or service, that is restriction of viewpoint, and if we ban discussion of the product or service that is restriction on subject matter. As we discussed earlier, some of these prohibitions are not about information but about behaviour, and the ban on viewpoint is designed to modify behaviour. Other restrictions are also designed to affect behaviour (as, for example, the ban on tobacco advertising). So, second, we have to consider what is normally labelled categorization: we ban certain categories of speech, and these categories are very carefully circumscribed in order that the bans on areas of speech do not become casually enlarged.

Other types of content on which there is general agreement about the lack of protection – or prohibition as we more normally would call it – include libel, bribery, espionage, obscenity, child pornography and direct incitement. We agree that libel should be prohibited, and we allow legal action to be taken by someone who is libelled. The others we usually regard as criminal actions and the perpetrators are pursued through the public prosecution system. There may be other areas but the list is not long, and some areas are slightly unclear. For example, there is a ban on product placement in UK television programmes, a ban that is upheld by the broadcasting standards authority (Ofcom), but there is no ban on advertisements that promote these products. However, should these advertisements make false claims then they are banned by the Advertising

Standards Authority, but there is no criminal prosecution and no private legal action unless a particular person is harmed by the advert.

The third area we should note is that there are costs if we are to promote free speech. You or I may be disgusted or outraged by particular TV programmes, we may be offended by certain claims, our reputation may be damaged by exposure in the media, or we may be distressed by publicity about private matters like divorce, bankruptcy or other court proceedings, but none of these should interfere with free speech. Where individual regimes or jurisdictions draw the line between what is acceptable and what is unacceptable comment is a matter for local debate, and obviously if you are drawing up information policies you should know where that line comes; Cohen's later arguments may help find that line. His arguments would allow us to litter the streets if that is the only way we can get access to the readership or audience. Effectively, at election time when we festoon telegraph poles with candidates' posters we are doing just that; most countries have requirements backed by penalties that the posters should be removed within a short time period after the election. That is a cost of the speech necessary at election time. A similar cost attaches to public figures: they must be open to more public comment – have less protection – than the rest.

Finally, and associated with this problem of costs, we should note the need for fair access. Once again, the assumption is that in a democracy we must ensure equal treatment and equal access, and we must understand that Cohen's arguments are for democratic societies. Information policy is serving an end, as we shall see when we consider Cohen's ideas about interests and vulnerabilities. We do not want to find that access to media, or the ability to speak freely, is concomitant with economic or social position – and that is why we must allow leaflets in the street. This need means that we really should not make content-neutral restrictions – people must be able to speak where they can. There is also a problem about unfair access associated with not just media power – the kind of power that Habermas complains about – but also where the material distributed is upsetting or disturbing for others. The common example of this is pornography, often said to degrade women. The idea that the answer to speech is 'more speech' is difficult to put here – is more speech the answer to pornography, when those who object to it may not feel they want to speak in public against it? Where power is unfairly distributed it is difficult to speak out against those in power. Think of the difficulties of speaking out in any institutional setting where power is unevenly distributed, and so distributed with general social consent, like a school, or a place of employment. Guaranteeing fair access is critical, and obviously it needs institutional support.

False starts

We noted the starting position with the minimalist and maximalist protections for free speech, and Cohen's proposal for another approach. We should note more fully his objections to the other approaches because he calls them false starts, suggesting that their explanatory power is too limited to form the basis for policy.

The minimalist approach – denying speech has a cost and suggesting that, anyway, we can't trust governments – has the consequence that any discussion about speech has to focus on other actions rather than the speech itself. Also, it does not allow us to make any moral comment about, say, pornography, for example, so we can't express preferences. This approach emphasizes the evil that free speech protects against rather than any virtue in any speech in itself. This seems very limited and does not allow us to be discriminating between various instances of speech, nor to count the costs of speech, which is potentially harmful and certainly disrespectful to those who have to bear these costs. So if you live in a society where left-handed people, those with red hair, those with black skin or those below a certain height are constantly derided, denigrated or despised, and you are one of those people, you would have to accept that such speech had no cost, and you could not seek redress, if we accept the minimalist account. This does not seem acceptable.

The maximalist position recognizes your cost, but does little more, saying that free speech must always trump other claims. In that position it does not tell us how to discriminate between acceptable and unacceptable costs of speech, or to tell us why we allow false political promises or claims to be heard but not false advertising claims. So, this approach too seems short of explanatory or analytical power. Cohen wants something that gives more value to expressions than the minimalist approach and is more discriminating than the maximalist. Structurally, Cohen's use of the other two positions gives him good grounds to put forward his alternative. From this initial critique of the 'false starts' Cohen builds a picture of the realities that any protection of speech must recognize. He draws us into a structure where we must recognize interests, costs and background facts. These constitute the picture of reality that he wants us to accept and from which we can then construct a new approach to the protection of speech. Effectively, therefore, his argument is a presentation about the nature of the world we live in and the needs we have if we are to operate successfully. So, rather than arguing for particular cases or particular societies he gives a normative statement of the 'on the ground' situation that any protection of speech must recognize. We will look at interests, costs and background facts in turn.

Interests

Cohen says we have three types of interest – expressive, deliberative and informational. The requirements of all three imply that speech must be protected. Cohen assumes that even where there are differences of opinion, these are reasonable differences in an environment where there is a pluralism of values and people can accept and debate with others whose values may be different but which are still reasonable and where there is some chance of people reaching a common ground. This is one of the great weaknesses in Cohen's argument, because we cannot always assume that such pluralism of values will apply or indeed that people will be reasonable with one another about differences of opinion.

Structurally, however, this is a useful device, because it draws attention to this requirement and forces the policy maker to employ another strategy if the reasonableness is not there. Cohen, however, offers no advice on what that might be. This means that we have to think of information policy for freedom of speech as being dependent on the assertions in the UDHR discussed in a previous chapter, or perhaps on some discussion that places information policy within one of the grand social theories that might require freedom of speech. Making arguments that justify protection of speech by appealing to interest may have to include some extra steps where there is no common ground or pluralism.

For the moment we will accept Cohen's claim and consider the interests that need protection through speech. First we will consider the expressive interest. This is just a recognition that we wish to express ourselves on matters of human concern. We might wish to speak out on a matter of political justice, we might wish to give testimony or a statement of witness about some event, or we might wish to speak through art, including as in satire when the subject is ridiculed but because we afford less protection to public figures the speech is protected.

The deliberative interest has two aspects, both of which demand protection for speech. First, it is reasonable for us when contemplating action to want to do what is best, and thus we must have the means to find out which is the best or most worthwhile, and what strong reasons support that action. Second, we must also be able to understand what those reasons are. This is what we do when we say we are deliberating about something. The 'something' need not be action, it could be the formation of an attitude, but in either case we need to be able to find out what possible alternatives exist and what support there is for them.

Finally, the informational interest covers the point that we need to secure reliable information about any attitude or action we may be deliberating over. This, and the deliberative interest, is covered in Article 19 of the UDHR, guaranteeing the right to seek and receive information.

Costs

Structurally, Cohen has now identified a set of requirements that lead us to demand the means to realize these fundamental interests, thus giving the impetus to protect speech. He now turns to recognize the costs associated with protecting speech and to offer a hierarchy of importance of various costs. This is a more searching examination of the costs question than was available in the two false starts. He itemizes three types of cost.

First, there are direct costs, where the actual words used cause the injury: the words are the cost, they do the damage. So, if you tell me that people of my skin colour are inferior, I am hurt by the words themselves. Second, there are environmental costs, where the expression does not directly hurt me but helps to create an environment where people like me are regarded as inferior, even if the expression did not tell me that I am inferior. Creating a climate by using speech is a very common practice in public life, so we are gently introduced to ideas like higher taxes, smaller pensions or reduced health cover through public discussion in the media. A similar discussion might be about immigration, and if it creates a climate where immigrants are regarded as troublesome, likely to commit crimes or welfare burdens then that is an environmental cost. Finally, someone might decide on the basis of things said to take some action against immigrants; this would be an indirect cost of the expression. Even though the expression did not enjoin any action, someone has moved on from the actual words to the next step, and this must be regarded as a cost of the expression.

Are we willing to bear these costs, and do we accept them all as costs of the expression? It must be that some expressions carry costs that we will bear because of the substantial points being made by the expression, and others we will not bear because the expressions are trivial.

The background facts

Having considered the costs, Cohen then turns to enumerate the background facts, which are the inescapable facts about the way the world is, the working environment in which we must fit and secure our notions of protected speech. These facts are complex, and they are the third structural element to Cohen's case. First, in enumeration of interests, he identified those points we would wish to defend for ourselves; second, in the costs, he identified, literally, what our interests cost our environment; and third, he lists the facts that we must accommodate, and which also give us reasons to protect certain speech.

Cohen is offering in his 'background facts' a representation of the way the world is which we may cavil at for its lack of correspondence to the world we know. We will immediately encounter what Cohen calls facts which we might want to label aspirations, although other facts he gives us are uncontroversial. What is significant for our general discussion of information policy formation is the use of this apparatus where some representation of the 'way the world is' has a role to play in the structure of the argument. This works in two ways. First, it gives us a basis from which we can argue what it is we have to do to secure the objective of protecting speech. Second, it gives us an idea of what we are facing, what difficulties we might encounter in securing protection of speech. Cohen gives us four types of facts: facts of reasonableness, the bare facts of life, the cold facts, and the unhappy facts – those which cause us some distress about the world.

The facts of reasonableness are, first, that there is a reasonable pluralism: with free speech people will arrive at conflicting but reasonable convictions and views. And, second, the fact of reasonable persuasion – that people can change their minds when they hear reasons presented to support a point of view different from their own. There are two points we can make here. Obviously, democratic societies depend on the assumption of such reasonableness, and depend on reasoned debate over public issues before legislatures or governments make decisions. Maybe you do too, in your work or your home; there is an unspoken assumption that reason works. However, we may object that, although reason works in most cases, those where we most need a well worked-out policy are precisely those where there is a noticeable lack of reasonableness. Conflicts around the world seem to fail on this point, and even away from those recent examples of divided societies like the Middle East, South Africa or Northern Ireland, even with relatively minor disputes over resource ownership and utilization, it seems that 'reasonable persuasion' is not in evidence, and that what counts is power. Power is one of the other 'facts'; that Cohen includes, so it may be that our unwillingness to recognize that there is a 'fact of reasonableness' is covered by some of the other facts. So, structurally, there is some resilience in Cohen's claims.

The bare facts of life are, for Cohen, facts of resource dependence, and facts of innocent abuse. Resource dependence recognizes that expression relies on resources that are usually unequally distributed. Some people own newspapers or TV stations; they find it easier to get their opinions known than you may do. Others may have not only no obvious access to some means of broadcasting their views or even any means of expressing them, but they may also lack the knowledge of how to secure some means of making their views known. You may think that you have no particular view that you want to air on television, but that might change: would you know how to express yourself? Can you afford to advertise? Can you command the attention of your legislature or government? Perhaps, in an equal world, everyone would have that possibility open to them, but otherwise those who have resources have an advantage, and the rest of us are dependent on someone else giving us access to those resources. We can also note that the resources are framed and formed according to the views of their owners: the TV companies decide what kind of programmes will allow public participation, and what format that participation may take.

The fact of innocent abuse recognizes that where speech is uninhibited, even when it is not malicious, some upsetting things may be said. When you, after keeping your opinion to yourself for too long, speak your mind, telling a few home truths, your listener may be devastated at the criticism they are hearing from you of everything they have innocently done. These bare facts, innocent abuse and resource dependence are just recognition that the world is a rough and tumble place. What we must decide is whether we just accept that or whether we act to correct it. The 'correction' could be restriction on speech, but if we accept the claims about reasonable persuasion we must follow the idea that we want to offer correction in the form of a reply – in other words, more speech. That objective brings us to confront the cold or chilling facts and the unhappy facts of life.

The first, the cold or chilling fact, is that people will be afraid to speak if they may be subject to some sanction for so doing. If a king says 'you can say what you like and I won't imprison you so long as I am not upset by your words', then no one will speak because they cannot know in advance what will or will not cause upset. Where people fear to speak on some issues, all speech is threatened and there can be no certainty that people will speak. More comfortable is a situation where we know that if some issue is of concern to people then they will speak and we will be informed, and then the facts of reasonableness will allow discussion. This suggests that far from being aspirational, as at first it might seem, the fact of reasonableness has a structural role within the overall framework of the facts of life which we need.

The unhappy facts are, unhappily, many in number. Cohen lists five: power, bias, disadvantage, easy offence and abuse. It may be that there are more. With these Cohen is emphasizing the inequalities and daily difficulties of life, showing that if we have a policy about protecting speech then we must contend with these perturbations to the smooth operation of the idea. The vehicle that conveys the right of free speech must have robust suspension to cope with these bumps in the road.

The fact of power is a name to recognize that most people do not like to be criticized and prefer to have agreement with their proposals, and accordingly will do whatever is in their power to avoid or suppress criticism. A child who has been taunted or bullied at school and who, having complained, finds that the actions continue will be loath to complain again. The same applies at work and maybe in the home. There are things we know we cannot say, not because we are wrong, but because we know that it will be the worse for us if we say them. A policy that seeks to protect speech must find some way round this operational problem: just proclaiming the right does not secure it in practice. The fact of bias relates to ourselves and our use of the power of speech to negotiate our way in the world. The bias here refers to our preference to persuade other people to do what we would like them to do rather than what would be in their own best interests.

The fact of disadvantage, as represented by Cohen, states that disadvantaged people in society tend not to prosper when speech is regulated by vague standards controlled by the more powerful. We are all familiar with circumstances where a particular form of words, and not some equivalent, is required. People who are inarticulate or who have difficulty stating their views succinctly do not get much air time on broadcast media, and *vox pop* pieces on television where roving reporters seek responses from people in public places typically frame the question. The citizen can only respond to the question put to them, and gets no time to give elaborate answers.

The fact of easy offence recognizes that, most likely, someone somewhere can be found or will emerge to object to almost anything; few topics are so anodyne that nobody has an objection to one view or another, and as the essence of protecting speech is to allow things to be said in contentious cases, it must be true that protecting speech requires us also to allow for objection. As discussed before, Cohen's answer is to provide for more speech rather than to prohibit speech. As with the previous 'unhappy facts' we have to ensure that speech is protected but also that it is not inhibited. Finally, the fact of abuse recognizes that where there is sharp disagreement – the cases where we particularly want protection for speech – then there is a natural tendency to seek some advantage by some means like shouting down opposing views, distorting or exaggerating facts, vilifying opponents, or otherwise seeking some advantage that does not rely on the meaning of the words used and adherence to the facts. The pretty picture of speech, which might remind us of Habermas's idealized public sphere of debate where reason alone could prevail and all participants could be heard according to the strength of their reasons, is difficult to realize in real everyday circumstances.

We need to pick up two points from this elaboration of Cohen's picture: first, the role of these facts in the structure of the argument – not just his argument, but in the construction of any argument about any aspect of information policy. Some recognition of the imperfect nature of the world is also recognition of the need to put in place protections for speech, and with this restrictions on the possibility of censorship that go beyond inhibiting official sanctions on speech to include positive mechanisms to protect speech that ought to be made and heard. Second, we can ask whether the particular points made by Cohen suggest that it is not worth all the trouble to protect speech. The answer must be that, for Cohen, the objective of protecting speech in a democratic society makes this worthwhile. If we want some justification for protecting speech in societies that may not be democratic we need something more. An appeal to the UDHR is, in such circumstances, unlikely to be successful, and military or other authoritarian regimes will typically allow only as much freedom of speech as is consistent with their maintenance of power – giving some force to Cohen's inclusion of all his 'Facts of Life'. Discussion of how to protect speech outside democratic societies needs more space than we have here. But we should note a small point about the structural role of the democratic ultimate purpose in the argument. There is a question whether this element can or should be retained in analogous arguments in other areas of information policy: do we need to recognize intellectual property rights in a democratic society? Can we construct arguments about such rights as a component of information policy using Cohen's structure or one similar to it, and if so does the democratic point have to be retained? We will return to this later.

Implications of Cohen's strategy

Cohen wants to emphasize the role of speech in countering speech. In a democratic society we want to talk through all issues, we don't want anyone resorting to other means – power or other coercive means – to resolve arguments or to govern speech. So, Cohen needs to show how the structure he has presented will meet the need. We will look at how content regulation, categorization, costs and access are affected by his claims. These are all critical matters in any discussion of speech protection. First we should note that Cohen emphasizes the deliberative and expressive interests and the need to protect them. He is emphasizing the value of expressions and their role in regulating and resolving disputes. Thus, speech can counteract the harms that speech might do, and he has to allow that there may be some minor harm because he recognizes the rough nature of life. His structure gives him the values he wishes to protect, because of his analytical recognition of the deliberative and expressive interests, and it also bestows the means to make decisions about content.

Cohen says that content regulation represents a direct threat to the expressive interest even when there are good reasons for such expressions, and people would be prevented from expressing their views. This must lead us to be wary of content regulation. Regarding categorization, where expression is banned in a small and clearly defined number of categories, Cohen suggests that we should make reference to the fundamental interests to get a sense of the importance of expressions. So, commercial speech – advertising and so on – is less important than political speech, because it is less connected to the deliberative and expressive interests. There is a positive advantage to categorization because it avoids *ad hoc* regulation, which might lead to a creeping increase in the range of speech which is regulated against. Use of the arguments about fundamental interests and the background facts provides a mechanism to determine what should be protected, with the assumption that where there are costs to bear 'more speech' is the remedy where the fundamental interests are too strong to warrant regulation.

There is still an argument to face about the costs of speech. Why should we bear the costs of speech? Cohen wants to say that where fundamental interests are involved the cost of offending someone is outweighed by the benefits bestowed by meeting the deliberative and expressive needs, so those offended by such speech should 'avert their eyes'. Those who are offended must bear the cost of offensive speech. He has more recently attacked the problem of terrorist activities and speech, but here we will stay with his original model because that gives us the coherent structure to work with. With other expressions we must weigh how important the expression is, how vulnerable it is to under-protection, given the background facts, and also weigh what harm it does. Cohen wants us to maintain a system where, if speech is important and vulnerable, we should protect it, whatever the cost, but where it is less important, even if the costs are direct, it is less worthy of protection. So, speech against public figures should be protected, but speech against private individuals may not be. This accords with our own instincts but gives a better rationale for them (protecting fundamental interests) rather than the *ad hoc* injunction that public figures should expect to be the subject of public comment.

It might be that we still face difficulties here, not because Cohen's argu-ment is inadequate but because we can argue about the nature of the facts. So, in the case of the fashion model photographed outside the drug rehabilitation clinic, there is an argument about whether she is a public figure or not. There is also a potential problem about the medium of expression. So, I have before me a cartoon showing in crude graph-ics a recognizable likeness of a political leader. The cartoon has this per-son saying words that, as far as I know, he has never said, but the effect is to make a satirical point to the government's disadvantage. Is this fair comment? We accept that it is because we understand the medium of the cartoon, and we accept that although there is no truth value in the words attributed to the leader there is an underlying truth value in the sentiment the reader is left with. For the arguments we have followed above to work there must be public recognition of the nature of certain media forms.

Finally, there are points to make about fair access. Fair access is part of the mechanism for meeting the costs of speech. To allow 'more speech' when someone is offended or harmed by some speech we must guarantee them fair access to make a response. This is particularly true for disadvantaged groups who might otherwise have no easy access to media to make a response. It is fair access that can secure the expressive interest, and the deliberative interest is also served by ensuring fair access, because the deliberative interest needs to consider all the possible actions open to someone, and therefore these must have had some expression in some accessible form to be available.

All these points are content-neutral, but a different set of questions arises when we consider content-specific regulation of speech and fair access. The classic example, which Cohen uses, is pornography, but we can generalize the case away from this specific example. If some speech harms people to the point where they are disempowered, certainly if they are disempowered to the point where either they cannot reply or that any reply they make will lack credibility, or because the act of having to reply to counter the specific speech is demeaning for them, then there is a problem about the whole system of allowing speech because more speech can counter any harm it does. If pornography demeans women they may feel they should not have to reply to it or that they are embarrassed or subordinated by having to reply. In such cases there would seem, extending Cohen's argument, to be some case to restrict pornography. If there is hateful speech against some ethnic or religious group the same arguments can apply. We might think that certain speech against immigrants would fall into a similar category. Cohen, however, has some problems with this, and we must be with him. Regulation that restricts the flow of ideas should not be permitted, so even if some speech is hurtful it should be protected.

Where Cohen countenances regulation is in cases of speech that provokes or stirs up violence – because that too, like the case of disempowering some group, acts against the process of regulating disputes and disagreement through speech. So, too, 'fighting words' may be proscribable. What may be required here is some element of sub-categorization, so not all pornography, but certainly obscene pornography, may be proscribable. This seems an exception to the general sense of Cohen's argument, but we can justify the proscription of certain sub-categories by appealing to his arguments about fundamental interests. This slight operational difficulty leaves open discussion about how wide the sub-categories might be, and that leads us to the final part of the review of Cohen's work.

Structural strengths

We are using Cohen's arguments to see if they can work, and that needs to be discussed at two levels. In fact we have four sets of questions to consider before leaving this question of censorship, free expression and free speech:

- We need to know if this argument is structurally good. Why do we need something so complicated?
- We need to know if the arguments are analytically useful.
- We must consider whether they are operationally useful.
- We need to know if arguments with this structure can be adapted and applied to other areas of information policy.

Cohen's model is certainly complicated, yet in our review of its components and how they would be applied it did seem that there is a role for every element that he introduces. Some of the elements he enumerates may lie open to discussion as to whether they are comprehensive: the section on the background facts may be in this category. There is no need here to propose alternatives but we should note that any attempt to transpose the arguments to other areas of policy will possibly need a substitute set of components at every stage. The weakness lies not so much in the structure but the assumption that people are open to reasonable persuasion. What do we do when events prove otherwise? We can proscribe speech but we cannot force people to speak, or to engage in dialogue. So, the 'fact of reasonable persuasion' may not always work in favour of extending the range of permissible speech and may fail on two counts: first, it will not allow the model to work as intended; second, it will allow careless extension of the regulation of speech. We are dependent on reasonable persuasion being a fact, but this may be less of a problem in other information policy sectors, where some willingness to engage in discussion is a prerequisite for any policy on the issue.

Analytic utility

The second question concerns the analytical utility of the model. Does this model help our understanding of the issues? Does it clarify our knowledge of what freedom of speech is and why we should protect speech? The model forces our attention first on the general purpose of serving the needs of a democratic society and puts the fundamental interests of individuals in a privileged position. Those fundamental interests are framed as being things that an individual needs in order to flourish as a member of a democratic society. We can ask, what if society is not democratic but there is still a need for a civil society to exist where people can operate daily autonomously without outside direction? Even in a democratic society where there is some understood social or political goal – some kind of national project that effectively meant that all people had to discharge their duties to realize this goal, and therefore lost much potential freedom of action because their fundamental interests would have to be shaped in line with the national project – would it be possible to apply Cohen's model? Such a situation would be close to some of the claims discussed earlier when we were looking at ideas about the information society. Other societies where this might apply could be those dominated by one ideology or faith.

Analytically, we can see that the model forces us to confront what the fundamental interests of any individual might, in an operational context, be understood to comprise. The same is true for operations within smaller units, like work groups or families. It may be that a particular family is working on several family projects, and family members are expected to operate within the parameters of those projects. So, a family could be working to bring up children in a particular way, build the family home along certain lines, establish its place within the community by certain actions and memberships of social groups, and make provision for older family members and for the old age of current adult members. Such an intersecting range of projects might require that family members, whatever their notional autonomy as individuals within the broader society, are required to reformulate their fundamental interests according to the constraints that family membership imposes.

Families, like work groups, tend not to be democratic societies, but the individual members can be said to have a role as autonomous democratic citizens in the way Cohen outlines, but also to have a constrained existence at another level. We can say that at the family or work group level the constraints are voluntarily borne because there is another possibility open if anyone wishes to leave the particular family or work unit and assert their rights as citizens. Where their rights as citizens are compromised to the point that they lack autonomy, then we can say that Cohen's model has a limited application because its claims about individuals can never be realized. Even within the state that corrals all its citizens into some national project there is an assumption that the subordination is voluntary by the individual. The point being made here is that the Cohen model does seem to have an analytical use, in determining how the fundamental interests are being understood, both at the level of society in general and at the levels of smaller sub-groups.

At the operational level the model also seems to be good because its components give a clear indication of where the pressure points lie. The application of the background facts allows us to build a picture of what individuals need. However, as a working model we must find that there are some problems. First, we have already noted the difficulty surrounding notions of 'reasonable persuasion'. There is also a difficulty in defining what exactly the threshold for hate speech is, especially as Cohen makes clear that offensive speech in most cases is to be tolerated. Another problem with the model at the operational level lies in the degree of acceptance it might receive. If you were to propose that, at work or at home, having previously used the model to analyse the level of protection for speech that is required, you were to propose that the model be adopted and the outcome of its application to be used as 'best practice', it might be that there would be outright rejection by someone who might claim that Cohen is wrong in saying that speech has a cost. Someone could reiterate the claim that words are just words and harm nobody and nothing more is needed.

There are several lessons that this gives us if we want to export the model, or at least its structure, to other areas of information policy. We will consider more detailed aspects of applying the model elsewhere; here we need to note some general points. We can itemize the steps for the model:

1   Current analysis of the situation in an information policy sector is inadequate and inaccurate.
2   Current operational practices do not meet the need or offer suitable protection.
3   Current levels of recognition of costs are too limited and don't help identify real needs.
4   We need better identification of fundamental interests.
5   We need better identification of costs.
6   We need better identification and analysis of the 'real world' situation and the constraints that imposes.
7   The working model needs to be able to work out difficult cases.
8   We need to be aware of the assumptions the model rests upon before applying it.

With these points in mind we now turn to another information policy sector, and this should be a sector that is different in character from the question of freedom of speech and expression, where the interests to be served are constituted in a different way.

7

Privacy and data protection

WE SHOULD BEGIN this review of information policy provisions for data protection by putting it in the context of social and government action. Unlike issues of censorship, which tend to be dealt with at government level and imposed largely at the behest of governments, data protection is an issue that gets its momentum from grassroots activism. We saw with Cohen's model for protecting speech that the main concern is over-regulation of speech, and that there are several issues relating to the character of the society that we live in that make it imperative to generate action to reduce over-regulation. Governments have a lazy interest in prohibiting speech – such action might reduce the risk of political dissent, and of discord and disruption of the civil order between sections of society, and it can protect the government's own interests where there is a need to protect national secrets or a desire to prohibit investigation of government action.

Issues of privacy and data protection are not matters of concern to government, except in so far as individual members of government have an interest in restricting public knowledge of and comment on their own actions. Beyond that the only government interest lies in ensuring a minimum of discord among its subjects or citizens, and by protecting data or recognizing privacy some small level of civil order may be maintained. Recent events in several countries, particularly the

UK, have shown that governments or their agents or agencies are lamentably inept at protecting data about citizens. Records of millions of citizens contained on computers or computer readable media have been lost, found in rubbish dumps, or stolen. Such records often include sensitive financial or health information that might expose those whose names are on the list to financial loss or other distress. Governments are not alone: banks, which also keep huge files of the financial details of their customers, have also lost such data.

In most societies the only agency with the authority and power to protect data is the apparatus of the state. This includes the promotion and passage of legislation; the establishment of oversight agencies and responsible personnel; and the identification of illegal acts, penalties, processes of redress and if necessary punishment, and codes of conduct to ensure the safety of data. Thus, the body that produces and holds most data about individual people is also the body most likely, on current evidence, to offend, and the ultimate locus of authority for securing and enforcing good practice and protection of data. Thus, governments have to police themselves, and police actions which are of no threat to themselves. That someone's identity is fraudulently misused is disastrous for the person concerned but no threat to the conduct of government.

Thus, there are several barriers to overcome. Government must be persuaded to take on extra functions at tax-payers' expense to police something of little interest to the authorities. Legislatures must be persuaded to pass legislation that is efficacious: it has to be precise enough to offer protection that can be enforced while not impeding normal exchange of goods and services. Promotion of this protection comes, typically, from citizens rather than from governments. There are four points we can note immediately.

First, technology has an important role in this. The records recently lost, mislaid or stolen were on easily transportable media or small personal computers. It is with the introduction of easily transportable data that the problem of loss and theft has multiplied. When records were in paper format in large filing systems with little chance of them being moved around any theft would have to be an intrusive act, breaking into the record store. Computers also offered the opportunity both to search large quantities of records very quickly and the chance to cross-check records in one file with those in another, a task that previously would have been very laborious. This process of record-matching poses other problems of trust independently of the extra issues raised by computer technology. A final point to note about the convergence of telecommunications and computers is that when data is transferred by cable or airwaves it is much easier to intercept flows of data, thus making it necessary to have enhanced means of encryption. It is possible, as it was not a generation ago, for someone to steal data without leaving home, and to misuse the data to their own benefit instantly, without actually making any change to the original data and with slight chance of detection.

Second, first-generation data protection laws only covered computer records, as it was in that area alone that problems were perceived. Only more recently have records in all formats in member states of the EU been covered by EU directives and legislation.

Third, there seems in many areas of life to be an operating principle that capacity to do something breeds the desire to do it, and this sometimes translates into a belief that there exists for those with the capacity a right to do it. So, we now have governments and other agencies seeking to collect and store vast quantities of extremely detailed information on large sections, perhaps even a majority, of the population. In December 2009 the British government was still pursuing the goal of issuing biometric identity cards to all citizens: these machine-readable cards can contain information that the card holder cannot see or read. The desire to record more information, notionally in the interests of protecting the country and its citizens from the threat of terrorism, has led to a wide increase in surveillance powers and record collecting, exacerbating the problem of data protection. Obviously, we have to have a policy about what information can be collected, about whom and how; who can access it, use it and change it; and what rights the data subjects themselves might have. Obviously, especially when governments want to keep secret the records they hold, of telephone conversations, for example, there is an interesting relationship between censorship and freedom of speech – when people are restricted from casual use of the records they have access to – and data protection, just as there is between legitimate secrecy and privacy.

Finally, we can note that the discussion tends to be about record collecting and the protection of that data, but there is the larger and related issue of privacy. Do you have a right to do things without intrusion by casually curious intruders or onlookers, or without the intervention of government agents, or without anyone else being able to profit from data about your life? Several jurisdictions have tried, or have considered, privacy legislation, with mixed results. That which is private extends beyond what is outside permitted levels of intrusion to include issues of property; people have property in their persons that they can rightly protect, so we find that along with issues of censorship, secrecy and freedom of speech, issues of intellectual property also relate to data protection and privacy.

The need for legislation

Experience shows that data protection needs legislation, as anything that lacks compulsion also lacks effectiveness. Too many organizations, agencies and individuals find data protection bothersome and expensive. As it is generally admitted that the vast majority of data transfers – estimates suggest over 90% – is completely innocuous and without threat or risk to anyone, it is easy to see that without the force of law it would be too tempting just to overlook requirements because the chance of any misuse is so small. Furthermore, where there is a chance to make money out of personal data transfers it could be very tempting to some people to ignore any law that lacks means of enforcement.

A simple example will illustrate the case. It is said that in certain US maternity hospitals women who gave birth would shortly thereafter receive mail and mail order catalogues from firms selling baby-related products. Someone in the hospital, or maybe the hospital itself, was selling names and addresses of new mothers to the baby product companies, without the consent of the mothers. It could be argued that it was to their advantage as they were given access to sources of products that they would need, but the point is that personal data about them was transferred without their consent, and without any control over what happened to that data thereafter. The temptation to act that way is strong; for many organizations a mailing list is a major asset, and selling it on to others can be a major source of revenue. What was once considered an innocent and maybe a helpful act (passing on the names of new mothers to baby product firms) now constitutes a breakdown in data protection. Why are we so worried about this, and why do we need to include this within information policy?

As was indicated in Chapter 1, the nature of modern life is one where we must surrender data about ourselves frequently and in greater detail than ever before in order to get services, products and assistance, or even just to participate in communal life and to complete everyday tasks. Tax, health, housing, educational, transport, welfare and financial services all require us to give personal data. In many cases this is just to establish or confirm identity, or to ensure an adequate level of service: it is quite in order for health services to ascertain information about us like our blood type or any previous medical history. We expect that this data, freely given, will remain confidential between us and the person or agency to which we surrender it.

If you go to the doctor and describe symptoms and problems, even if they are not extremely personal or embarrassing, you would be very upset and astonished if you happened to visit some public place like a bar and you found your doctor discussing you and your private details with other people. Implicit and understood rules about confidentiality would have been broken. On the other hand, if the discussion had taken place in a professional setting, say in a hospital, you might be glad that your doctor was getting additional advice, and you would assume that the rule of confidentiality was not being broken.

Confidentiality

There are conflicting interests and practices that we need to disentangle if we are to understand how information policy about personal information and data can be set. In particular, there is an important question to settle about the utility and effect of confidentiality. The practice of keeping secret certain information may be in the interests of the data subjects, but it is also true that professional groups benefit from the exclusive knowledge that they hold. Confidentiality as a doctrine and practice may be of more benefit to the receiver of the information (the professional practitioner) than it is to the giver (the data subject). This can be especially true if treatment or service will be determined on the basis of the assessment of large numbers of individual people.

So, to clarify some of the terms we have been using, you expect details of your life and actions to remain private, unless you determine otherwise. This is the essence of privacy. The information you give to others about yourself you give with the understanding, usually, that the information will not be handed to others and will be guarded with some care. This is confidentiality. Any such information that becomes a data element in a record about you, or in a record system about many people, you expect to be treated with respect and to be kept safe and free from inspection by others. This is data protection.

Unfortunately the situation is usually more complex. There is some general acceptance that some degree of public disclosure of some private information is in the public interest. The difficulty lies in determining what the proper limits of such public disclosure might be. First, we have to accept that the value of privacy is one that is accepted, that there is no valid assumption that anything and everything about somebody can legitimately be made public even if they do not consent. This is not a matter of information policy, but more a question of our notion of the person and the construction of society. However, how much privacy someone might claim may vary between jurisdictions and through time or according to national circumstance. As a rule, in western societies we expect that should someone be accused of a criminal offence that fact will become public knowledge, as will details of the subsequent trial and, if there is a conviction, any sentence that is given. This matter is partly a question of the public at large having knowledge of transgressors who might constitute a threat to the life of others, but it is also partly because we need to have some public knowledge of what is being done to people by those with coercive power; the publicity that should attach to government action will also mean publicity about certain people, and this implies some surrender of privacy.

We also require, as part of the process of constructing communities and having knowledge of the status of people in them, declarations about marital status and responsibility for the rearing of children. Additionally, and somewhat urgently in an age of extensive travel, we need to know about people who have infectious diseases. But there are questions about how extensive this process should be. For example, recent developments require people convicted of sex offences to sign the sex offenders register. Such people will be known to the police. Parents of young children may feel that they have a right to know if sex offenders live in their neighbourhood, or if children of people with AIDS attend the same school as their own children. Our current practice is not to release this information generally. Privacy is an elastic concept, but we have to be more certain about the way data is protected.

The problem becomes more complex when we consider not just information about individual people but also information about corporate bodies, like companies and organizations. Furthermore, we have to determine the relationship between privacy and data protection and levels of government secrecy. Corporate bodies are a difficult question, especially commercial companies and organizations, because typically they collect and hold information about general market conditions, including the activities and plans of their competitors. Disclosing such information to the corporate data subjects would be to reveal commercial intelligence, so most corporations are extremely reluctant to reveal which other companies' activities, products and future developments they consider commercially significant for themselves.

This neatly expresses a more general point that relates to all of us. We need information about other people in order to conduct our daily business: just as we have to surrender information about ourselves we also have to collect it about others. Most of this collected information is innocuous and innocently collected, and is rarely stored, most of it being used and discarded instantly. We rarely think of ourselves as collecting information about others, but if you give one moment to think of all the contact people you have listed in your mobile phone for your convenience and which may be in your possession for several months or years you will understand the level of casual, and innocuous, data collection. If you have links to a variety of social networking software applications you will also either be collecting information or at least linking to an extensive web, much of which will be invisible and unknown to you. If you ever find that your e-mail suffers a security breach and a hacker is able to plant a message in your system that is automatically sent to everyone in your address list, and thence on from theirs, you will have a stark illustration of the problem. We all live in an interconnected world of information exchange and data sharing, and computer and telephone communications exacerbate the adverse aspects of it.

Problems of power

Even information that we freely give in necessary exchanges passes through several systems and may cross jurisdictions. Every time you fly out of the country there is an international data transfer, and although mostly it is harmless there is, for example, a current stand-off between the USA and EU over air passenger information. In the USA a different regime pertains: anyone can collect any data, and if one party is harmed they can seek redress through the courts. This means that everyday vast quantities of personal data is exported from EU countries to the USA where it will have very few of the protections that are seen as essential in Europe. The US authorities have said they will encourage all data controllers to follow 'best practice', but that no law can be applied to enforce this, and if anyone does not like the situation they can stay out of the USA. This is a clear example of the coercive nature of many data transfer activities: any time you seek a bank loan you will have to surrender information that you may feel obliged to give in order to secure the loan, but which you may feel is too intrusive and not wholly necessary.

In both the air travel and bank loan instances, most likely the data transfer is without problem, but when there is a problem, through misidentification or identity theft for example, the problems are immediate and immense. Getting a correction and redress is time consuming, possibly expensive, and meantime you may be unable to travel or withdraw money from any bank. When the data record about you is either out of date or otherwise inaccurate the problems can intensify.

So, the overall problem is that we have to have some set of principles that regulate this activity, and which are also effective operationally. The operational question is complicated by the way information can be used once it is accessible. You may think that information is about you and attaches to you as an individual, but it can be used by others in two ways. First, it allows other people to determine group membership, sometimes in ways unknown to you (for example blood tests can help health officials identify the group of people with certain medical conditions, or bearers of infectious diseases), and – quite obviously in the case of the medical example – that can enable people to act, both by giving them the information they need (for example, who has got this particular disease), but also giving them the authority (by identifying that the number of people with a particular virus constitutes a public health problem) to act. In this instance the information conveyed about group membership is relatively innocent, and we can presume that its use is in the public interest (even if it may inconvenience you if you are quarantined).

Second, the information that is being transferred may be used as a bargaining or negotiating asset, by being withheld or used selectively. This too is largely innocent – you give your phone number or e-mail address to only a subset of the people you meet, but it can also be exploited, by people with knowledge of how data is used, to personal advantage and perhaps the disadvantage of others (by withholding information about a virus you have, or by creating false information about yourself as you make a declaration for a record that is to be entered in a record system, for example, by misrepresenting your income when applying for a bank loan).

Information can be used selectively in conjunction with others to form coalitions to obtain a working advantage. From this point springs the power that certain groups, particularly professional groups who hold personal data about others, are able to exercise, partly because they have the power that the information gives them and they are able to match it with other cases known to them, and partly because the ideology or professional state of knowledge they have will effectively authorize them to take particular actions. Lawyers and doctors are key examples, but the point also applies to public servants working for governments and government agencies, where knowledge of government plans and negotiations plus the detailed mass knowledge of information about the population as a whole gives them a group advantage by the selective use or release (or refusal to release) data.

We are in effect building up a picture similar to some of Cohen's 'background facts' that can help build a model for the analysis of data protection. Rather than attempting to build that here we should note more of the operational conditions and comment on the choices that lie open to us when determining policy in this area.

General questions

A first question to ask is, should we be concerned at all about data protection and privacy? We noted above that privacy has to be an elastic concept, and we could take the view, rather like the minimalist position for freedom of speech that Cohen rejects, that data is just data, it does no harm by itself, and we should allow whatever data collection people want to do. Echoing the maximalist position that Cohen also dismisses we can say that if there turns out to be some harm done in particular cases then that can be dealt with as a normal issue for the legal system, there is no need for expensive and cumbersome special provision. Furthermore, in support of this, we can say that it is just not possible to secure for people the traditional right of privacy, the 'right to be let alone', because, as has been discussed above, the world has changed. We have to surrender information to get benefits and services anyway. Connected to this position we can ask whether, in the name of increased efficiency, we should abandon any restriction on governments and their handling of data. If most data handling is innocuous and governments can probably do things in secret anyway, why burden our systems with extra regulation, sacrificing instead a little personal privacy for much more efficient government, unconstrained by special rules about personal data? When discussing human rights and information policy we considered whether a contrary but legitimate position would be to organize information policy to suit the needs of government, and by abandoning data protection we would be fitting in with that.

Against this position we can make three points. First, the most spectacular recent cases about the loss of data have included many involving government agencies – taxation, health and armed forces. Whatever may be the merits of allowing governments to handle personal data freely there needs to be some provision to secure data against loss, unless we are prepared to abandon completely any attempt to maintain any level of privacy. The loss of data relates to a second point, which is that if there is out-of-date or inaccurate data in circulation it can act as misinformation in the system. Just as data subjects (the people who the data is about) need protection, so too do data users need to have confidence in the data they are handling, so there is a good case, whether or not we invoke some need for security about data, to maintain a system that ensures the accuracy of data. The third point here is that most problems with data – over its storage and security, its collection in the first place, its accuracy and its use or misuse – seem to relate to governments which are anyway the users of the largest amounts of data. So provision to secure against casual misuse or opportunist abuse of data seems critically necessary.

As data subjects are at a disadvantage compared with data users or controllers there is also a need – invoking some of Cohen's points about the background facts and the need for fair access – to build in security for the data as protection for the data subjects. In unprotected systems data users can use the data more or less as they feel the need and can sell it on or casually dispose of it without regard for its security. This constitutes a potential problem for the data subject who may have no knowledge that data has been passed on and may be used for purposes it was not originally intended for. Actually it is also in the interests of third party data users that the data is accurate, as well as in the interests of data subjects needing to secure against uncontrolled use. So, there seem to be good reasons to have some kind of data protection regime in the interests of fair commerce as well as protection of subjects.

The alternative is to make radical adjustments to our views about privacy. This would require us to put social and community considerations ahead of individual claims for privacy, but even if we had no concern for individual privacy we would still need to have regard for the quality of data that was put into general use, so we would still need a data protection system. More importantly, decisions about the concept of privacy are not information policy decisions, so we must accept that the concept exists and that it has high status in most western societies and in many others too. Information policy has to work out a data protection solution that meets the expectations about privacy even though the concept is not legally defined or part of the law of many countries.

There remain two other general problems. First is the question of the doctrine of confidentiality, closely related to the idea of privacy and central to the professional ethics of many occupational groups dealing in human services. Second is the problem posed by people's enhanced readiness to disclose information about themselves and give others access to it through social networking applications. Confidentiality we will return to later: the social networking phenomenon has not yet evoked well-worked-out responses by information policy makers or by data protection advocates, whose main concern is with large record systems of systematic information about large numbers of people – credit card records, for example. The social networking sites do not make any substantial change in data practices; they merely make identity theft easier if social network users decide to offer detailed personal information. This puts more pressure on policy makers to include secure technical and administrative systems to secure data, and creates a greater need for users of social network sites to have a greater personal awareness of data protection problems and secure data practices.

The world of data transfer is somewhat similar to a card game played by several players, but with one crucial difference. In a card game using a standard 52-card pack of 13 cards in four suits there is a finite set of cards, so when four of any value card have been played you know that there are no more to come, whereas in real life there is no limit on the number of data records, with limitless variations in data in them. In a card game we have a hand, our own cards, and we can guess at what our fellow players have. Sometimes we can make inferences from the way the cards have been played, or from the bids players make about their chances to win, so even when we don't have complete knowledge about the cards we can, from the information we do have and the inferences we make, put together a fairly complete picture of the game. So, data protection must protect people by having regard for what total picture might be gleaned by possession of partial information, and by putting in place appropriate systems.

It is the task of information policy to have regard for the overall attitude towards privacy and confidentiality, to have awareness of the threats to data, both in terms of its vulnerability to capture and the dangers attaching to that capture, and to work with what requirements data protection principles impose and what constraints and possibilities the various technical and administrative protective measures can achieve. These fairly mechanical operational needs can be plotted against an analysis and assessment that might be fashioned along the lines offered by Cohen for freedom of speech.

The principles of data protection include concepts that have already been mentioned:

- Openness: there should be no secret files.
- Participation: data subjects should be able to find out about records, see what is in files held about them, and see how data is used and by whom.
- Collection limitation: data can only be used for the purpose for which it has been collected (and data can only be collected when the purpose has been made clear).
- Use limitation: data can only be kept for the time and purpose for which it is needed.
- Disclosure limitation: data cannot be passed on without the consent of the data subject.
- Information management: records should be correctable.
- Accountability: any person or organization collecting, creating, holding, using or disseminating data is responsible for its accuracy.

Putting principles into effect

How do we give effect to these principles? A first point to answer is just what types of personal data can be included in the area of protection. It would be an immense task to subject all and every collection of records of personal data to regulation, and as most data is not a problem most jurisdictions set limits on what must be subject to regulation. Usually all information is subject to the legislation, and all data must be held in compliance with approved rules, but much data is specifically given exemption from registration. So, the membership list of names and contact details of your local tennis club is not really a problem – if you are an office bearer of the club – but you must still observe the rules about the use of the data, so you cannot use that list to canvass for votes at a political election, or sell the list to someone else. Nor can you keep a list of potential members of the club, and someone outside the club has no business keeping a list of names and addresses of members. Can you then keep a list of the team members of your favourite football team who played in each game last season? That seems not to be a problem and the information is probably available over the internet.

The internet raises another set of questions, as data can be hosted externally to any jurisdiction and personal data could be given on a site with little chance of restricting it without taking action against the internet service provider. What we can say is that when data sets or records cease being innocuous they then can be considered to come under the provisions of the legislation. The trouble is that most malicious uses of data are not advertised. When they take the form of identity theft the offence is usually against one individual and does not constitute keeping a record system, so it is a different form of offence. The data protection complaint would be against the record system that had not properly secured the data. When data is sold on as a commercial asset it is most likely not made public, and when in-house abuse of data occurs – using the data for a different purpose than originally intended, keeping it longer than is justified, failing to keep the records up to date – the incident or failure to observe principles or legislative requirements is probably not known at all.

This highlights another problem with data. In the case of censorship or the failure to maintain free speech the fact is usually directly known and can, generally, be made widely known as a restriction on speech. It is thus relatively easy to mount a campaign to correct the wrong done. You can broadcast – on your website, in letters to newspapers, or on the news media – that you wanted to say 'X' and have been banned from doing so. In the case of data protection problems you will not want to broadcast the information you are seeking to protect, and no one else can know the specifics of your complaint, only that some protection has been breached. So, there is a publicity problem about data protection. In the case of censorship there is usually a direct or close relationship between the speech affected and the state apparatus; in the case of data protection the state may not be directly involved and also reluctant to bear the expense of action. So, we also have a potential enforcement problem with data protection. Even where there is an effective working mechanism to implement sanctions against offenders there is still the problem of data that lies outside the normal range of the mechanism.

These points show that the information policy planner has crucial decisions to make to secure personal data while still sustaining legitimate data use. Privacy is recognized in the UDHR, and data protection is in Branscomb's list of information rights. However, we must remember the provisions in the UDHR that make rights a means of creating and sustaining communities, and subject to the need to maintain public order. We could take a view that privacy and data protection should be set so community needs are met, even if that meant curtailing data protection. However, earlier we saw that the concept of privacy has to be accepted as it is outside the control of any information policy planner. So, the information policy agenda is partly predetermined, but the process of finding appropriate mechanisms is still ongoing. Various countries have settled on different solutions. It is generally agreed that for data protection regimes to be effective they have to be legally binding and must have an enforcement mechanism. But what is to be enforced, and how do you set the punishments so that those with something to gain will feel the punishments are an effective deterrent? Paparazzi in France face fines of 60,000 euro, but this does not work as a deterrent: the prices they can get for pictures make the fine bearable.

There are two factors to take into account here. First, the legal framework, including the mechanism to secure compliance (a major problem) and the structure of penalties, must be effective and fair. This is something that we can use some adaptation of the Cohen model to determine. The other factor is the administrative process, and the record so far is that there are at least three variant examples of process available to us. The US preference is to offer redress through the courts and to make no restrictions on what data anyone can collect. If some harm results the victim can use the courts. This is administratively efficient and places minimal burdens on government. But victims may not have the means to use the courts, and they may not know they are victims if data misuse is skilfully concealed. A variant is the Canadian model, where a government-appointed commissioner oversees the successful administration of laws protecting personal data, but the process of using the courts is maintained.

An alternative is offered by two European variants. First, the British and Irish require the registration of data controllers (people who keep the record systems containing the data), and set rules for data users and protections for data subjects, and offer through a data commissioner a free mechanism to pursue breaches of the law, seek correction of records and improvements in systems, and secure redress for victims. Registration sets no limits on who may collect data but does require declarations from data controllers that they are holding records. The variant of this, which we can label the European model, requires data controllers to be licensed, establishing a potentially tighter level of control over data collection and use. It is not clear that the Cohen model, which might be adapted to give an answer to the question of how much data protection we need, can help in determining the administrative process. We do know that the EU regards levels of data protection in the USA to be inadequate, but, as explained earlier, there is little that the EU can do: people want to travel to the USA and the USA is a sovereign state. That clearly shows how difficult it is to secure and enforce adequate levels of protection over personal data.

8

Freedom of information

FREEDOM OF INFORMATION is about improving public access to government information. It is different in character to data protection and also to censorship and freedom of speech. We should be clear about the terms we are using, as there is often confusion between freedom of information and freedom of speech and expression. We might also include 'intellectual freedom' in this. Intellectual freedom is a term similar to freedom to read but being more inclusive and covering more, and concerns the right to read or view as we wish, without censorship. Freedom of speech and expression are the right to make utterances without censorship; they are obviously closely related to intellectual freedom and the freedom to read.

Freedom of information is different, although it does relate to restrictions on the right to read, as it is the name given first to campaigns, and latterly to laws, to enforce governments to release for public view information they have collected and hold. The matter of increased government secrecy has become a major issue in the last 30 years but has been the subject of campaigns for much longer. The cause of the concern is familiar: the increased volume of government activity, the extension of government action into many more areas of life, the effect of nearly a century of wars or near wars for most of the advanced industrial nations with the attendant paranoia about national security, and increased democratic concern about the accountability of those with power. The movement to increase government accountability is, like the movement to secure data protection, pursued from the ground up, and, as with data protection, the legislation was resisted and then introduced with reluctance. The difference is that in the case of freedom of information the legislation is aimed solely at the governments themselves and for its implementation is dependent on government goodwill and willingness to reveal what information it holds. The information is of two broad types, which overlap: the information governments collect, and that which they generate from their own work – the working documents of government.

The reluctant introduction of freedom of information has been matched subsequently by an incidental battle over its efficacy and continuation, by direct attempts to repeal the law, attempts to include exemptions in subsequent laws, attempts to frustrate its operation by simple noncompliance, under staffing of freedom of information offices, and the charging of fees. Although many people feel that few countries have freedom of information laws that go far enough in enforcing disclosure it is agreed that some areas of state activity are legitimately exempted from the provision to disclose. Defence, negotiations with other states (but not the outcome of the negotiations: there can be no secret treaties or clauses to treaties), negotiations over certain financial matters like setting national interest and tax rates and the processing of contracts, and police operational planning all seem consensually exempted. Where the actual working boundary lies between that which is legitimately secret and that which should be disclosed varies between states and is a matter for political negotiation. Sometimes citizens of one country may seek information like satellite pictures from another country, even when their own country refuses to release the information. Striking the right balance is a matter for information policy.

Confronting governments

Obviously, we have to contend with many of Cohen's background facts in confronting freedom of information, most obviously the fact of power, as freedom of information campaigns must be conducted against governments themselves. In this case it seems that we have, as with other issues in information policy, a particular difficulty over the competing claims of academic analysis and campaigning for change. We need to be clear what the basis for seeking increased access to government held information might be, because it most obviously is not an information question but rather a question about the nature of government.

There are claims that government can be more efficient, and needs to be efficient both for the country and in the interests of taxpayers, by not being subject to freedom of information laws. These laws, to be effective, mean that any and every government department and agency, and every other public institution covered by the law, must maintain documentation systems that give any legitimate claimant access to any document to which they are entitled, and do so within a reasonable period of time – usually a matter of a few weeks. This action obviously has a cost, and as every relevant body must be compliant with the law they have to employ a member of staff, usually called a freedom of information officer, and maybe a team of such staff, possessing administrative, legal and technical competencies. Along with claims about impairment of efficiency, the cost of implementing and maintaining freedom of information is frequently given as a reason for not implementing such laws. The justification for that claim is that so few people 'legitimately' ask for information that the whole system is a grossly excessive provision for a minor and infrequent need. 'Legitimately' is given in quotation marks because there is a claim that many of the requests received under freedom of information legislation are by people who are not within the groups originally identified as needing access to such information. So, instead of politicians, journalists and citizens, the information is being sought by corporate lawyers, and sometimes by criminals. The suggestion is that, yes, there is a cost if some people who need access to this information cannot get it, but that is a small cost to pay compared with the vast expense of sustaining a massive system just to give businessmen cheap access to possibly privileged information.

Two other complaints about freedom of information that we should note concern actions to reduce the impact or avert the application of freedom of information laws when they would be, by any normal reckoning, considered necessary. The first concerns commercial misuse. There is a story that the chief executive of a US minerals exploration company noticed that in the interest of air safety all flights, including small aircraft flights, from all airports would have to be logged with the US Federal Aerospace Administration (FAA). He realized that such reports, which would include details of routes to be flown, would be available under freedom of information laws, and thus that commercial intelligence about his company's operations would be freely available to competitors. He lobbied successfully to defeat the proposed implementation of logged flight reports for small aircraft. This meant that crashes could be more difficult to locate and victims less likely to be found alive. We would probably think that the safety issue should outweigh the commercial interest.

The other issue is that of government willingness to co-operate. Freedom of Information requires a level of acceptance by governments and its agencies. Usually with cases of censorship there is some knowledge that an item is being censored, either one specific item or a class of items (for example, soldiers' letters home in wartime). We can see with freedom of information that we could have virtually no knowledge of the existence of individual documents or even classes of documents without the active involvement of the government agency involved. We have already mentioned that subsequent legislation may seek to exclude parts of government from the requirement to meet freedom of information laws; we also have to consider that where any government activities are handed to subordinate agencies or outsourced to private companies these may not be covered by the legislation either. There is plenty of opportunity for government to evade the intentions of freedom of information legislation, and we know from the history of several states that public servants and politicians can find they have a strong interest in assisting that evasion.

Building commitment

All this may excite our indignation, but the lesson for analysts of information policy is that we can't always rely on information policy, or any appropriate legislation, being an effective instrument, capable of compelling compliance, by itself. In earlier chapters we talked about strong and weak theories of information policy, and also of information policy in certain circumstances operating autonomously. When we look at individual sectors, like data protection or freedom of information, we see how policy can be effected through the operational instruments, and the effectiveness of these must be considered when making statements about the strength of theories. If we accept that the legislation, although requiring compliance because it is legislation, may yet not be followed to the letter because it is convenient to ignore it we are just confronting a reality. The background facts that Cohen identified come into play here, especially the 'fact of reasonable persuasion'.

We are forced to accept that the only mechanism forcing compliance in freedom of information policy is the commitment of the public servants operating the system, and working in the government departments and agencies, to abide by the spirit of freedom of information. That effectively means that they are committed, intellectually at least, to an understanding of freedom of information within information policy that probably relates to one or another of the overarching theories about society, like the information society or the idea of the public sphere, which in turn engages them with the spirit of information policy. Alternatively, at a lower level, they may consciously just have a commitment, or a willingness to accept, open government. This may mean that they would accept a strong theory of information policy but that they would not see it as autonomous. This really underlines the point that particularly for freedom of information but also for information policy in general we do need to recognize and work with the point Cohen identifies as 'reasonable persuasion'. This suggests that it is worthwhile constructing an approach to freedom of information using the Cohen model.

Constructing the case

We already have many of the components, some of them direct adaptations of the model Cohen developed for freedom of speech. Because some level of government secrecy is accepted (and this extends beyond state secrets at national level to the range of items that must remain confidential in local government), we already have room for varying stances about how much information should be made available. Obviously, there are those who will say that freedom of information is unjustifiable, but the general debate at present is about how much information should be public. So, we can mirror the argument about minimalist and maximalist positions. It could be argued that information is just information, and that it is better to have maximum disclosure of state held information and that there are no costs associated with this disclosure. It is also possible to state very plausibly that even if we accept that there are costs associated with the release of state information it is better to bear this rather than face the potential costs of letting the state decide what information it might want to release, whatever the citizens might decide. This would be the equivalent of Cohen's maximalist position. It is also easy to argue that neither of these is satisfactory, precisely because they do not help us determine where to draw the line on release of state held information. Currently in practice that decision is made by establishing within each jurisdiction some sustainable consensus, which reflects international practice, jurisdictional requirements and political expediency. This is almost like making *ad hoc* decisions, and, subsequent to the initial legislation decision making about what extra to include or exclude as new state agencies are set up, the practice is also very close to being *ad hoc* in many jurisdictions. If we want information policy to be strong we have to find a better set of arguments, and we would also like to develop a form of procedure that would lead to supportable decisions in this area of policy that would also make information policy stronger and more compelling.

This is almost a test case for information policy in general, because it is the one area that is almost entirely about the state and dependent on the state for implementation. Whereas engaging the state to act as an agent for the effective introduction and maintenance of policy in almost all other areas is a challenge, in this area, and also in respect of freedom of expression, campaigners for freedom of information need a logic that is compelling enough to enforce compliance. If we are acting as analysts rather than campaigners the effectiveness of freedom of information need not concern us but we can still use the Cohen model, or an adaptation of it, to secure an understanding of how policy works, or fails to work. The Cohen model, or rather our adaptation of it, is then not just a tool of analysis that leads to decision making about policy, but also an aid to academic understanding.

What we cannot learn from the analysis is what the policy is for. We might accept campaigners' objectives to secure maximum access to officially held information, or we might accept the objective to strike a balance between the interests of potential data subjects (the population) and data controllers (the state), and we can work out how these might be attained, but we cannot from the analysis get a sense of what the overall purpose and intention should be. The process that we can complete at this level of operation is the technical one of determining the correct mechanism to bring about the practical policy guidelines we seek. We can go through the steps identified at the end of Chapter 6, and for convenience those steps are reproduced here, and show how they can apply to freedom of information.

These are the steps for the model:

- Current analysis of the situation in an information policy sector is inadequate and inaccurate.
- Current operational practices do not meet the need or offer suitable protection.
- Current levels of recognition of costs are too limited and don't help identify real needs.
- We need better identification of fundamental interests.
- We need better identification of costs.
- We need better identification and analysis of the 'real world' situation and the constraints that imposes.
- The working model needs to be able to work out difficult cases.
- We need to be aware of the assumptions the model rests on before applying it.

The inadequacy or possible inaccuracy of freedom of information analysis we briefly discussed above, when we took two positions (on the one hand that information is just information, that there are no costs attached to it, and that there is no impediment to maximum disclosure of state held information, and on the other that we accept the costs but they are, ultimately, a lower cost than allowing state apparatus to determine what should be made public) and reflected that current policy debates are about how to determine a balance between an operational interest in secrecy and a public right to know.

In relation to the second point above, that current practices do not meet our needs and do not offer suitable protection, we can say that adherence to a principle of open government, or of a principle of every citizen's right and need to know what his or her government is doing, does not identify what should remain secret. That leaves us in a situation where every decision about what should be public will be a political debate between adherents and opponents of freedom of information, because we have no mechanism to identify for us where the boundaries of state secrecy are to be drawn. What we can say is that there are interests to consider on both sides (let us for these purposes think of an adversarial relationship between government and the general public). Furthermore, we can include with these interests some calculation of costs. Clearly, governments as major producers and consumers of information also have an interest in promoting their own policies and actions, so they are inclined to do whatever they can to present their actions in the best light, and will want to ensure that the publicity machine of government is tightly run so that all messages emanating from the government or its agencies are in line with the overall government information strategy. This is what we have come to know as 'spin'.

Questions of model building

This would seem to be something similar to Cohen's expressive interest. There does not seem to be an equivalent on the other side: the expressive interest of the public is closer to that we saw protected by Cohen's argument about freedom of speech. However, there is a deliberative interest of the public that needs access to government information and which should be protected, along with, obviously, the informational interest. The public has an interest in the maximum disclosure of state-held information, and this, along with its deliberative interest, can run directly counter to the expressive interest of the government.

Is this a good way of describing the conflict that arises over freedom of information claims? It may not be perfect, but it is an improvement on what we had previously. An illustrative case arose recently in the UK, where a sensitive document was disclosed by a civil servant to a member of parliament (MP) who also happened to be the opposition party's official spokesperson on the relevant topic. The government, or its agents, employed the police to search the home and parliamentary offices of the MP and to arrest and detain him for several hours. This was done legally, because although no warrant to search the premises had been obtained the police had secured the consent of parliamentary officers. However the issue became a political storm because, since the 17th century, parliamentarians have enjoyed immunity from arbitrary search. An enquiry established that the police action was 'disproportionate', and that the leaked document would merely have embarrassed the government, rather than being a threat to national security. Here we can see the government's expressive interest being privileged over the public's deliberative and informational interest. Can we construct, or do we need, some hierarchy of interests? It would be difficult to do so, and might operate to the disadvantage of some group. We need to employ some other criteria to determine the relative claims of government and public.

Here the other parts of the model's apparatus assist us. We can identify costs. In the case of the MP it might be argued in a blanket way that the privileges of parliamentarians must always trump the claims of government, in the interests of protecting the freedom of parliamentarians to act and vote as they feel is right (otherwise they would always be in fear of government intervention and their arrest). However, it might be the case that sometime an MP really did act against the national interest, in which case we might argue that it would be right to search his offices to protect, say, national security matters. How do we allow this without also allowing the government to plead this case when it does not really apply (as in the recent case mentioned above)? We can apply not only the idea of costs, but also the idea, taken from Cohen, of background facts, in particular the 'fact of power'. We should give prominence here to the 'fact of innocent abuse'. In this case the abuse is by the government against both the MP and the concept of parliamentary privilege.

With the arguments about the background facts, which, as with the last mentioned fact of innocent abuse, we have to adapt to the different circumstances of freedom of information, we can build a better picture of how to make decisions about the balance of interests between the general public and the government. In the example discussed above it was the government's expressive interests that were at issue, but we can also see that there is a strong argument to say that the government's deliberative interests are also at stake here. In an argument more normally expressed as a claim about government efficiency we can see that it is easier to operate in government if you have confidence that not every little aside or discussion paper is going to be released publicly, leading to claims for explanations and attempts to intervene in the process of government policy making. Governments need to deliberate about their actions, and just as citizens need information to make the best choices of action so too do executive authorities, be they governments or commercial organizations. If the process of deliberation before decisions are made is public we can see two processes at work. First, there will be delay as intervention extends the time needed to make a decision. Second, to cope with this, the *locus* of power retreats. This means that the decision making process is removed to a point that can evade public scrutiny, possibly in a way that makes government processes more cumbersome (and less efficient).

Competing principles and pressures

How do we counter this? Efficiency in government can be counted as a cost, but we should probably not seek to elevate efficiency to the point where it becomes a central principle. The Irish parliament adopted freedom of information legislation in 1997, but the Irish government forced through an amendment in 2003, which among other things sought to protect cabinet minutes from disclosure for an extra five years. This was to keep from public view documents relating to the sensitive issue of Northern Ireland. The Irish government's amendment was keenly contested at the time, but there is a defensible claim that the cost of exposing sensitive material relating to an ongoing issue, where lives might be at stake, is a smaller cost to bear than the alternative. If the argument had been that the Irish government would have been more efficient by excluding cabinet minutes from public view we might say that cost really was not significant and that the public's deliberative and informational issues outweighed claims of efficiency. Indeed, we might want public access to information about government actions so the public could see if the claims about efficiency were justified.

The claim that a sensitive issue justifies withholding information echoes the provisions in Article 29 of the UDHR that allows exceptions to the rights when public order or morality is at risk. However, if we just accept arguments and claims casually we have no process and are dependent on *ad hoc* decision making. An adaptation of the Cohen model would give us a checklist of the process that would determine what to make public. Just as with Cohen's original argument about free speech, we would have a presumption in favour of releasing information, without making the case that all government information had to be released. Famously, the British Official Secrets Act of 1911 prohibited the release of any unauthorized information, including, it was said, such incidental detail as how many cups of tea civil servants consumed. We might say that we are not concerned whether such information is released or not, just as we might not really be bothered about the practice of spin that coloured the process of releasing government information in Britain in recent years, as long as we can get at the information we feel we need. If 'spin' effectively suppresses or distorts information then we may want arguments to show that public access to information trumps government claims to present it at its own convenience. The final point in the checklist for our model, the awareness of the assumptions on which the claims are based, can be met by allowing for this presumption of openness – and most freedom of information debates discuss the idea of open government – but we can also take account of any theories about either the nature of society and its needs, such as information society or public sphere arguments that we discussed earlier, and arguments about human information rights.

We can see that 'real world' cases must confront issues of power more frequently in freedom of information issues than in the other examples we have looked at. Coping with the real world cases is put more severely to the test in these cases than in others because we rely on the government's willingness to participate in its own monitoring. We also rely on governments putting in place the effective machinery to ensure that freedom of information requests can be met. In the case of data protection the requirement that there be some enforcement machinery can be met by either allowing action through the courts as an ordinary common law case, or through provision of services through an information commissioner. In neither case does the government have to do anything, except pay the expenses of the commissioner's offices and activities. With freedom of information, where access to government held information is the issue, we need assurance that we can get that information within a reasonable time frame. This means that all government documents must be organized within a storage and retrieval system that facilitates rapid identification of relevant (and only relevant) documents and gives access to them. This is simplified in an electronic document universe but it still presupposes an organization that can access anything, whatever we may decide through argument are the documents that we should have access to, because the character of that argument may change through time, or even if the argument does not change the documents it leads to might increase or decrease in number, or be a different subset of the total, as understanding of the issue evolves.

Hence, as an additional expense requiring considerable staff time – the efficiency and costs argument resurface here – all government activities must be prepared for access to any and all of their documents. The processes will be familiar to librarians and indexers but they require that the indexing process is carried out across all parts of any government agency, thus adding to the costs as everyone must be familiar with the 'practice manual' for freedom of information. There are two points to put forward here. First, this might be good office practice anyway, improving the efficiency of government rather than impeding it. Second, the difficult case of getting government to participate in monitoring itself is facilitated by the requirement that all government activity should conform to the freedom of information practice manual and make annual reports on the levels of activity, including increments to document stores, indexing, requests and provision of access. This means that implementation is easier to check.

There is one more sector to consider before we move away from these micro level discussions of information policy. Intellectual property issues loom very large in any discussion of information policy, and in connection with issues of copyright they are of major interests to librarians. But for this discussion we need to consider the intellectual property area because it represents another distinct area where governments and individuals have different, and possibly competing, interests.

9

Intellectual property

INTELLECTUAL PROPERTY is an area of interest because governments have a different set of interests from those of citizens, and citizens themselves have conflicting interests according to the role they are playing. Citizens can be both consumers and creators of intellectual property, seeking to protect creators' rights while simultaneously anxious to secure the widest possible access to products. Governments, acting also as both producers and consumers, do not have the same interest in protecting creators' rights because they are not dependent on the income. Governments do have a secondary interest in creators' profits because they may enjoy tax revenues from the creator's work or from by-products of it. Successful creative activity leads not just to books, films, paintings, other art and performances, but also to merchandising – the T-shirts and mugs – that mark an increase in economic activity and hence tax revenues. There are two other secondary government interests. One is concern that they may be pilloried for failing to protect both the economic interests of living artists and the rights to access that the mass of citizens wish to enjoy. The other is concern that the activities of artists may effect a disturbance in the political balance, as art often criticizes power, especially when the exercise of political power against those unable to respond evokes satirical artistic comment. What better way to guard against this than to ensure that artists are enveloped within the

established system of national and community rewards and have maximum opportunities to create new work and to distribute it, while at the
same time ensuring that the population at large has easy access to this
work through the provision of free public libraries, museums and art
galleries, and subsidized theatre performances?

This concern for the living artist and the art-hungry citizen may be
the popular image of talk about intellectual property, but the reality is
different, and the reality of government interest is different. Intellectual
property law protects all intellectual property, not just that which can
be labelled artistic. So, all new knowledge, all scientific work, all engi-
neering and architectural realizations of new inventions and discoveries, and even all repackaging in new forms of existing knowledge (such
as school textbooks), is covered by law, international treaties, and national
and international organizations. This links intellectual property very
closely to ideas about the information society and the knowledge economy, but distances it from some conceptions of the public sphere where
a free exchange of ideas is expected. Intellectual property has moved in
our understanding away from being a public good whose creator needs
some protection to being perceived primarily as an economic asset that
can be bought and sold like any other product. So, we are talking about
trade, and the greater volume of trade in intellectual property is not in
new poetry being sold in small circulation magazines at provincial book
festivals but in pharmaceutical products, new information technology
software, and new industrial processes, and in the licensing to other industrial interests of these developments.

The informatization of all aspects of life, and not just those parts concerned with trade in new knowledge or skills, means that the information policy analyst and policy maker must be concerned with intellectual
property, and must understand it not only from the viewpoint of creators
and consumers but also from that of traders in such property. To that we
must add the primary government interest in setting up a regime that
encourages new creativity, particularly in tradeable end-products, by
protecting the creators, or at least the owners, of intellectual property,

while also offering maximum access to it. If this type of property, the development of new expressions or new inventions, is so important, why do we leave the reward system to the market? Would it not be better to intervene in some way to reward worthy inventors while making their products widely and cheaply available? In an earlier chapter we put forward the hypothetical case of an inventor who discovers the cure for AIDS (or for some other equally life-threatening ailment) that afflicts the poorest more than others. Is it not in the public interest to take this work and make it freely available? The inventor could be paid off with a large reward and society could be the owner of the cure to one of its most alarming problems.

Indeed we do have a system of alternative rewards in place. Most countries have academies of science, rather like the British Royal Society, membership of which is conferred on the most distinguished scientists of their generation by the recognition of their peers. There are also international rewards, such as the Nobel prizes, and a host of literary prizes that often carry financial rewards as well. At a more mundane level we have, in some countries at least, a system of Public Lending Right, whereby book loans from libraries are recorded and the authors of the most borrowed books receive a financial reward in proportion to their loans, but whereby also the rewards are capped at a certain level and any surplus the most popular authors may have earned is set aside for scholarships and bursaries for the most deserving new literary talent that may be struggling to reach its market. In this system we are rewarding both market success and perceived worth.

However, as mentioned above, the big money in intellectual property is with industrial developments and products. The scientist who discovers the cure for AIDS might be working for a pharmaceutical company that has invested millions of pounds in a ten-year programme to develop a drug to cure AIDS. Such drug development programmes cost much without any guarantee of success. Even if a scientific solution is discovered it may not prove possible to develop a commercially marketable drug, and even if the drug is developed it may not prove possible to sell it to its intended market. But let us say that the drug can be developed and sold: the company that produces it may have another programme of equal cost that is failing to produce results, and the costs of this programme will have to be recouped through the profits of any successful programmes the company has.

The market reward system

From the viewpoint of the information policy analyst the interesting point here is the involvement in the market. The other aspects of information policy that we have discussed all worked around relatively simple political or administrative issues – to censor, to protect data, to release data. None of those required commercial calculations. With intellectual property we are working within markets, with the involvement of very large commercial organizations, and their trade or professional bodies, and in a trans-national environment where the actions or wishes of one government may not sway international practice. What guidance do we have in developing policy? We should also note that the historical element in this is particularly strong here, in two ways. First, past practice cannot just be jettisoned: action is cumulative and must move with the awareness of the frameworks that have come from previous activity. Second, new developments, particularly in technology but also in trade patterns, products and organizations, may introduce such completely new conditions that the past provides no support but the need for swift action cannot be ignored. Indeed, companies may refuse to market products that are ready if the legal and administrative environment is not right.

There is, then, some pressure on governments to produce the right environment in appropriate time. When attempts to create the right environment fail, or no attempt is made, there is a disturbance in markets and trade, and uncertainties reduce confidence in the intellectual property regime. The situation is complicated by the wide range of types of intellectual property, the difficulties of distinguishing them, and the equally

wide range of rights associated with their production. A generation ago
Ann Branscomb summarized the potential complexity in saying:

> design of the laser disc may be patented; the process by which it is manu-
> factured may be a trade secret; the contents of a specific disc can be copy-
> righted; the commercial name under which the product is marketed will
> be a trademark; the talent whose performance is captured on the disc will
> be subject to performance rights; and the work, if retransmitted by a cable
> system, may be subject to royalties.
>
> (1988, 44)

We can add to this the rights associated with computer software, with
databases, and the newly emergent *droit de suite*. To these we can also
add the complexity that arises when a product is made up of components which are themselves owned by several different intellectual property holders and which may be in different stages of the exhaustion of
rights, and also the added complexity of products being made for specific markets under licence. It will be useful to go through the list of different types of intellectual property and discuss what problems are
associated with each of them.

Recognized types of intellectual property

The most well known types of intellectual property are those protected
by copyright and by patent, which are normally thought of as literary
works and inventions. We are accustomed to think of the copyright of
a work lying with the author, but although that has been established for
over 200 years it was not always clear that the author owned the right.
Recent practice has allowed authors to add a statement of claim to the
moral right to the work as the author is the real creator. But it is common for authors not to own the rights to their work, or at least to share
the rights with publishers or employers. A university, as employer, might
argue that an academic work is not just a product of the author's own

brain but is dependent on access to all the facilities, including libraries, laboratories and colleagues, that the university provides and that the work was written in time that the university has paid for. Authors may dispute these claims but universities commonly lay claim to ownership of the work of their academic staff.

Other authors, working for large organizations, may not even get their name on the documents they produce. Civil servants who write position papers for their political masters, or write government reports or draft legislation, might even be surprised at the idea that they could have a claim to the ownership of the work. Similarly writers of manuals for equipment would rarely expect to be credited. Where teams of people are responsible for a publication the claim of any one person is correspondingly reduced. These comments apply even more strongly to documents that lack the permanence of the printed word. Radio and TV programmes might give credit and recognition for the authors of complete scripts, but material that is essentially ephemeral is less likely to gain any recognition for the author.

Formerly, that is from the invention of printing up to the late 18th century, it was not clear at all that authors could claim ownership of the works they wrote. Ownership was more likely to be claimed by the publisher and printer, for the very good reason that they took the obvious commercial, and sometimes political, risks of publication. The publisher and printer (sometimes but not always the same person) might also claim permanent copyright in a work, so the printer and publisher who first published the works of an author could claim the right to print this work in perpetuity, to the exclusion of all other publishers. It is strange that what we so readily accept today, the limited extent in years of copyright, should be so well established. Any other product you make and own is not taken away from you or your family (more strictly we should say heirs and assigns) after 70 or so years. If you 'make' a garden that has a kind of signature to it that identifies the garden as one of yours, and if that garden is worth preserving through several generations, your heirs may have to pay tax at the death of each owner according to an estimate of the financial value of the garden, but they will not lose exclusive rights to the garden at any time. This will be partly because they have no such exclusive rights. A neighbour could like the garden so much that he or she could make an exact copy of it without hindrance. On the other hand owners of copyright do not have to pay any tax at the author's death on the notional financial value of the work.

Our acceptance of a form of protection for authors that gives exclusive rights to profit from the work, and to control the form of the work and the form in which it is published, is partly recognition of the role of the author as creator and partly recognition of the need to protect the author's means of livelihood. We also limit the ways in which other people can enjoy the work. We don't let them profit from the work without the author's consent and we don't let anyone reproduce a likeness of the work in another medium. If you liked a book you read so much that you decided to make a film loosely based on the book, so loosely that you decided to give it another name, you could be infringing copyright. Just how far should this right extend? There are some general rules of thumb which stipulate just how much of a work can be reproduced without breaking the copyright of the author, but some interesting legal decisions show how that principle extends or is reduced according to the circumstance.

One case concerned a retiring American president, a man of long standing in the US Congress House of Representatives, who came by accident to the presidency of his country. One of his first acts as president, and by far the most controversial, was to grant a presidential pardon to his predecessor. Once retired from office he wrote his memoirs in a book of great length that his publisher arranged to be published serially in a newspaper. However, a rival magazine publication somehow acquired and printed a short 400-word extract from the memoirs that contained his comment on the one interesting aspect of his presidency, the pardon for the previous president. An extract of 400 words is a very small part of the total work, so how could publishing it be considered a breach of copyright? On publication of the extract the newspaper cancelled the contract to publish the memoirs serially because the one element likely to arrest their readers' attention had been disclosed. The book publishers stood to lose a lot of money on the project, sued the magazine, and got judgement in their favour. The centrality of the extract to the whole work was a critical factor.

Another case showed that you don't even have to copy something to be in breach of copyright. A firm running special courses to prepare candidates for graduate admissions tests sent some students to take the tests, but not with any expectation that they pass. These students had been hired to memorize the test questions and then reveal them to the firm running the courses so they could prepare their students more effectively as they would know the real questions. The organizers of the tests had to scrap the test and devise a new set of questions as the original test had been compromised. The firm running the courses was in breach of copyright, even though nothing was copied. Other cases show the law to be less effective at protecting copyright owners. The financial services industry is notorious for the easy copying of ideas. A firm introducing a new 'product', like a new mortgage package, will probably have about three months to get as much business as they can before some rival firm will introduce a similar product. Similarly the clothes industry offers little protection against copying. Sometimes the copying is on a very large scale – as was the case a few years ago when the EU finally moved against the importation of cheap 'copycat' jeans, which were undercutting major designers' prices. Clothes are easy to copy, and even easier to nearly copy. A designer of swimwear found that a mass market manufacturer was producing garments that were similar enough when viewed from a normal distance but when seen close up were of inferior material and slightly different design and pattern. The case for infringement of design and copyright was lost.

Policy analysis questions

For the information policy analyst several questions arise. At a straightforward working level, where we are concerned to protect livelihoods, creators need protection, but apart from the wording of the law or international treaty some other considerations come into play. Although in recent years there has been greater emphasis on the rights of consumers there is still a problem about general attitudes to the price at which material can be had in the market. So, if some computer software is considered to be overpriced, particularly if it is also considered to be almost essential to have a copy for various types of work but especially for study, it is more likely that people will willingly use pirated or otherwise illegally copied versions of the software. The provision of 'student' editions of software at prices just a fraction of the commercial price are an example of a commercial response to the loss of business through piracy. This commercial response is not one that can be required by law or built into any policy on intellectual property, but the policy must recognize the existence of these cheaper editions. Typically, the trade-off for the availability of such editions is a call for tighter policing to cut down piracy. The popular music industry in recent years has seen prices tumble and traditional sales formats lose market position as music became available cheaper via the internet and as downloading free copies became easier. The attempts to pursue individuals and companies that break the law on copying have been startling but insufficient, and an appeal to the moral sense of users has also been employed to protect songwriters, performers and what we whimsically call 'record labels'.

The information policy analyst has a problem with these commercial moves, and with the moving sea of illegal or semi-legal market activity and the responses to it. Does information policy have a duty to protect any one group, be they consumers, producers, creators or even investors? Should we worry about whether music needs are met legally or illegally, as long as there continues to be a supply of new ideas and new music? We might have a general concern that all activity should be 'legal', but we can assure that by simply changing the law to include all current activity as legal. What is obvious here is that, unlike other areas of information policy where a change in the law could effectively alter the regime in, say, data protection or freedom of information, no such confidence can apply to intellectual property.

The situation is even more problematic in respect of industrial intellectual property. This area includes designs but mainly centres on patents. Patent protection exists for inventions that are new, original, necessary and workable. Every year very large numbers of new patents are filed. The situation is now becoming easier for inventors with more or less standard and common international registration of inventions and the international recognition of patent protection from any country. Until fairly recently inventors would have to file for patent protection separately in every country in which their product might be sold. As securing patent protection could cost as much as £50,000 few were able to get themselves the 'all-round' patent protection that would secure for them the ownership of their product.

What is patent protection, and how does it differ from copyright? The often remarked distinction that most clearly separates them is the difference in requirements and cover. Copyright conveys protection for the expression of an idea: patent protection protects a tangible product or process, the working expression of some new idea. Furthermore copyright will not give exclusive rights over anything other than that particular expression. Anyone else could express a similar thought or idea in a different way and get their own protection. Just because you write a collection of love poems you don't get copyright over the idea of love. Obviously, there is plenty of room for debate and manoeuvre over how close a distinct product might be to an original. Plenty of other 'like but not the same' questions arise. If you publish a paraphrase or an abbreviated version of a well known work, what can you protect? These issues are well known and answers are well worked out, but they are the result of negotiation and practice rather than any independent logic.

Rules and practices

The question for the information policy maker is whether to follow the practice or to devise instead a new rubric that either produces a similar result (and if so, why bother), or produces a new regime. The regime of intellectual property protection that currently exists, although notionally taking into account the interests of all parties, consumers and creators, is really a workable and working agreement with international consent to a broad framework with variations at national level in the detail. As an analyst or policy maker you may wish to develop an understanding of how the overall system works and what system would ideally be in place to produce an ideal environment for the development and exchange of intellectual goods. If you did that you would have to gain the consent of all the interested parties, who may be unwilling to countenance further change, particularly if it disturbs market arrangements.

Patent protection requires disclosure to ensure protection. The disclosure takes the form of registration of a claim, with supporting documents and examples, and inspection of the product or process. You thus must give up any secrecy about your invention, and anyone else will be able to inspect the patent awarded to you. There may be several reasons people would want to do that. They may want to buy your patent (they may even want to buy or hire your services along with the patent); they may wish to see how closely their own work mirrors yours – trying to see why you got a patent and they didn't; they may be wanting to develop your ideas by adding on some further work, or some separate item that would make much more sense, or make for easier use, of your own. They may even wish to contend that you have infringed patents they hold. You are thus entirely dependent on a well functioning system for the recognition and protection of patents. If the courts impose trifling penalties for infringements, or take too long to resolve disputes, the public will lose confidence in the system.

Alternatively, if the protection is so watertight that patent holders have an absolute control over the use of their work, and could in theory keep new knowledge and processes from the public in order to protect their own already existing but older and less advanced products, the public would again lose confidence in the system and the temptation to infringe patents would be strong. Similarly, if patent holders refuse licences to others who want to build the same machine or use the same process in other markets, or to add their own additions to the patented device, there is a further restraint on trade. As a policy maker you may want to encourage rather than restrict trade, and you must have regard not only to the grand idea, the consent of the public, and the willingness of inventors to seek protection, but also to the good working of the patent protection system.

Sometimes inventors think the patent protection system is too weak, offers too little protection, is too cumbersome or expensive, or offers protection for too short a time, and they will seek to keep their work secret, selling only the finished product. This might be difficult with machinery which can be taken apart, but where a process is involved and the end-user sees only the finished product it might be feasible. There are flow-on consequences of such a system, which have an effect not only on the exchange of ideas but also on the mobility of people with expertise, especially where that expertise involves secret knowledge. It would not be uncommon for employees to be required to sign agreements not to disclose at any time, even after the end of their employment with that enterprise, any of the knowledge gained in that employment. This obviously impacts the marketability of any such employee, and could be seen as another example of restraint of trade, in this case of labour mobility. However, where there are trade secrets not protected by patent there is also the possibility of industrial espionage. A thief could take a trade secret and, if they had the necessary knowledge, seek patent protection for it themselves, thus depriving the original developer of their work. Can you patent stolen work? This is an issue that a well worked out information policy would seek to exclude, even though trade secrets in general have little or no protection.

Copies and originals

The whole point of intellectual property regimes is to protect against theft. In the case of some tangible product like a house or a boat the case of theft is easy to detect, by determining who has possession of the item. Typically information products and processes feature easily reproducible items that are not diminished by copying, so the act of copying does not deprive the original owner of their work, but it may deprive them of revenue from it. There are obvious exceptions to this – works of art for example – but in general this point holds true.

Your wall poster of a well known piece of art does not constitute a copy of the original and the photographic wall poster has little or no financial value compared with the original. We do however move into interesting territory when we consider artistic fakes, especially when the market value relates not to what you can do with the product (you can use a computer program to prepare a book for publication), but the intrinsic merit of the work itself, either in conception or technique, or materials. In this case we are considering value as pertaining to the intellect that produced the work as much as to the work itself. (The art market is also distorted by the involvement of investors who are interested in art primarily as speculation or as a place to store money.) If some hitherto unknown Leonardo da Vinci work surfaces it will command a huge price in the art market because of the cultural association we have with the artist. If the work subsequently turns out to be attributed to a Leonardo 'school' its value will be depressed, and if it turns out that it is a later copy by an art faker then the value will evaporate. Why should this be, if the faker is as good an artist, in technique, as the original? Obviously, we reckon a faker or copyist to lack the originality and genius of the first artist, and we reward intellectual work in devising processes and machines in the same way.

A subsequent copy of a new machine lacks the flair of the initial development, and the millionth copy may be a representation of the original work but it is not that work. (Thus, broadly, we do not extend to copies or fakes the protection we accord original work. Intellectual property protection does not extend to an item, but controls that relate to the original recognition extend to copies, so there are limits to what you can do with a copy. In some cases we don't even consider these aspects.) We do not buy the latest version of some word processing software because we admire the way the code has been written or because of the way the developer integrates the use of sub-routines. Microsoft Word is unlikely ever to be regarded in the same way as a work of art, and we do not hear of early items of computer software commanding large sums in the marketplace. Software is likely to be a short-lived consumable item, and in fact we recognize it as such by giving it a shorter period of protection than normal copyright. Databases, similarly, enjoy shorter protection, quite logically, for the intellectual work they represent is largely one of compilation. In fact, computer software pricing seems to work in inverse proportion to the age of the product. Much art, of course, loses all value very quickly, but the sought after items seem always to accrue value with age, whereas computer software commands the highest price on its release. The problem with art prices creeping upwards with time is particularly a problem for living artists, and the *droit de suite* has been introduced in some jurisdictions to help them.

This new right echoes copyright in giving protection to artists for life plus a number of years, but imposes a new financial duty on art markets to pay a royalty at each sale to artists or their heirs and assigns. The extra cost of art that this implies has given rise to objections. Some critics say that this will act as a dampener on art markets on jurisdictions where the *droit de suite* applies and that art vendors will remove sales to places where the right, and therefore the extra cost, does not apply. Another claim is that only successful artists will have their work sold in major markets at high prices and they are likely to be well rewarded for their work anyway and that the new right will not help struggling artists. A third claim is that markets are arbitrary, volatile and capricious, no real judge of an artist's worth, and that alternative means of recognizing and rewarding deserving artists should be found.

Policy responses

What is the right information policy response to this? One response would be to seek universal application of the right, so all art markets would have to bear the costs equally. But even this would not meet the objection that the market is a poor way of recognizing good art. The information policy maker is confronted with the reality that the market, for designs, inventions, literary works and art, is the means we have for allocating rewards. Finding an alternative would be difficult and would probably face even more difficulties in getting accepted. There is also the problem of how else we would recognize merit in intellectual work. Hettinger discussed this and found no obviously feasible alternative to the market, even when the shortcomings of the market are accepted. Criteria for reward like worth, effort, labour, desserts, risk, cost and utility all give rise to difficulties, and an added problem is the point at which judgement is made.

Suppose a body of esteemed authors made the judgement that the works of J. K. Rowling, or perhaps of some other successful author, lacked the merit that would mark those novels as real literary creations, and therefore the author should receive no or little reward. At what point would the overwhelming sales figures force a reassessment? Do the large sales mean we must recognize merit in these works, and reward the author in some additional way? A relaxed response would say that we just recognize the nature of their production – that is that they are literary works and therefore entitled to the protection that we give such works, whatever their merit or success. This policy recognizes but does not privilege the market, but does nothing for authors whose work ought to be rewarded. Is it the task of information policy to do more than regulate the market and to intervene, to make judgements about the products in some way? Should we reward medical inventions and discoveries more than we reward the development of armaments?

In part these are moral questions, and that raises another issue close to questions of information policy. When discussing freedom of speech we considered arguments, particularly Cohen's that relegated work that did not meet our needs or interests to a lower level of protection. Pornography would be in that category. Yet the way we have discussed intellectual property protection pornographic publications are as entitled to protection as any other, and even when we disapprove of work we still allow it to be rewarded. Other moral questions are generally avoided. For example, we now feel differently about tobacco products from the way we felt a generation back, and in many jurisdictions tobacco advertising is banned. Yet older films show major actors smoking, reflecting the practice of the time but also the investment in the industry by tobacco interests. Should we now ban those films if we don't accept tobacco advertising; should we still allow them to make a profit?

These considerations about intellectual property and its protection illustrate the problems of the policy maker in this field, and show that several factors, most particularly the influence of financial markets, make policy generation more complicated and also make it more difficult to apply anything like our adapted version of the Cohen model for discriminating between good and bad claims for policy protection. We must also take account of the involvement of other actors in the formulation of intellectual, property protection policy. The other sectors we reviewed all focused on the relationship between the individual and either the state or some almost equally powerful organizations. In regulating intellectual property the state will want to secure the interests of both creators and consumers, and their relationship, but it will also want to ensure that its own interests are protected. In advanced societies, and especially within any society that conceptually or analytically is an information society, there is a need to encourage the production of new ideas and inventions, so policy must encourage, allow or produce the conditions that favour such endeavours. The favour needs to be extended to include the dissemination as well as the creation of ideas and inventions.

Conceivably a society or state could either discourage new ideas or be indifferent to them, and in such conditions intellectual property policy is easier to manage because it is concerned solely with the management of the market interests of creators and consumers. In a society where new ideas are needed there is also the consideration of how they will be rewarded and how they can be disseminated. In a world that was less jealous of property ownership it would be possible to imagine that new inventions could become public goods and the interest of the creator would be limited to gaining social recognition, maybe even fame, and also some adequate but limited financial reward.

In part these differing conceptions of how society should treat its inventors and authors can be seen as the equivalent of the first stage in Cohen's model, which we earlier abstracted to be rival statements about the understanding of the issue. Once we have this structural equivalent in the argument we can continue to use our adaptation of Cohen's model, as the later considerations like costs, background facts and so on can be structurally the same, even if they need to differ in detail. What is extra, and is critical, is some way of analysing and accommodating within the model the way the financial market will work. This implies too a greater attention to the detail of the policy mechanisms and an awareness of how they must work, because as we saw earlier ineffectual mechanisms will interrupt trade and therefore the production of ideas. Intellectual property policy is thus important at two levels – the way it works, and the way it gives expression to overarching conceptions of the role of information generation and exchange in society.

Part 3

Conclusion

Part 5

Conclusion

10
Final considerations

WE HAVE REVIEWED both macro and micro elements that influence the determination of information policy. There are other issues that we could have considered, most obviously the matter of how to determine the use of goods in common – that is, those that are limited in extent and which we all share. The broadcast spectrum is the commonly cited example of that. We have also taken the whole discussion from the viewpoint of a democratic society with a stable but powerful government and bureaucracy subject to some level of accountability to voters and legal procedures. Our discussion has also assumed that we are dealing with societies with effective, enforceable legal systems that are binding on all members of the society. The point about the law is threefold – first, that everyone lives 'under the law', second, that the law is an effective instrument, and third, that the spirit of the law that dictates the way the law is used is benign, reflecting a belief that law can be used as an instrument to bring about beneficial social change. The belief in the beneficial influence of law as an agent of social change has been available to us since the Enlightenment, but that view of law does not pertain in all societies, and in some instances law is still just an instrument of coercion.

Information policies in non-democratic societies

What do we say about societies where these points do not hold good? We can distinguish three types, which may not account for all instances but which certainly gives us some initial assistance in dealing with non-democratic societies. First, there is the case where the normal institutions of a democratic society living under the law have broken down. In this case we can appeal to some previously held intention or understanding whereby although the prospect of immediate restitution of former values and practices is remote we can at least work with the spirit of those and gradually move back to a normal democratic environment as other conditions improve. Second, there is the case where these values never did exist and the apparatus of government is weak and lacks moral and effective coercive authority. In these circumstances the chances of developing any kind of consciousness about information policy are slight, and the chances of getting enforcement of legal decisions is also probably slight, so issues like data protection and freedom of information are unlikely to be dealt with satisfactorily, censorship is probably arbitrarily but inconsistently applied, and intellectual property rights would be difficult to enforce.

In such an environment, with no stable and predictable exercise of authority or application of law, the chances of maintaining steady levels of freedom of expression or intellectual property rights are slight but the daily experience may be volatile, with police and other authorities acting capriciously, so it would be impossible to say with certainty what was protected and what was not. The third type we can easily identify would be those societies with hierarchic authority structures where the sovereign power exercises authority and coerces behaviour in its own interest. Such states would be absolute monarchies, military dictatorships, or ideologically or religiously bound states. In such circumstances all acts would be measured by the extent to which they served the sovereign or effective power. No rights-based conceptions would carry any weight and individual protections of the kind we have discussed in the last chapter would most likely not exist. However, such states do have effective mechanisms to enforce laws and regulations, and there would be information policies, probably rigorously enforced, that served the interests of the state. For example, there would probably be a very effective regime of censorship. Thus information policies can exist in non-democratic states.

In reality a state rarely fits clearly into any of these three types. Many states will subscribe to what we might loosely describe as international democratic values but be unable to guarantee delivery of them, except maybe in major towns and cities. Even if they can enforce observance of those elements of information policy that relate to the apparatus of the state it may not be possible to enforce them against the wishes of major private interests such as very wealthy citizens, the members of the government, very powerful international corporations, powerful neighbouring states, or powerful internal organizations like the church or the army. However, even here there will be information policies but we must learn, in our analysis, to determine what actually exists rather than what formally exists or what is merely aspirational.

In these instances, where information policy is confused, chaotic, serving arbitrary power or just disintegrating, should we really be concerned? For the information policy campaigner the answer is most certainly yes, because there are battles to be won, rights to be extended, and stable conditions to establish. For the analyst too there is much value in studying these cases, because they can illustrate most clearly several critical points, such as the limits of information policy mechanisms, the necessary conditions for policy to be effective, and the variation that might exist between the 'ideal type' information policy in democratic societies and the reality as experienced in so many parts of the world. Such societies also offer the policy analyst good material for identifying why we need information policies. If we extend this to tie information policy to education policy, which is critical for many developing nations, then analysing and understanding information policy becomes important in all types of society and states.

Against this picture of the types of political entities we are dealing with we must put two other considerations. First, the task we confront is putting information policy together, and it should be possible to do this for any environment, even if the prospects for immediate success are slim or the policy proposals initially seem unrealistic. The problems that unstable or unfavourable environments create remain problems of analysis and implementation, but the problem for the policy developer is to develop appropriate policies for that environment. That will depend on a number of the macro level considerations raised in Part 1 of this book.

Non-state information policy

The second problem remains more problematic, and can actually cause additional problems. Throughout our review and discussion we have concentrated on issues at national level, but many people have to generate information policies at a different level, possibly for the family, or for a community organization, more likely for a commercial or other corporate body. In Chapter 1 we put forward the proposition that anyone may have to confront the information policy issue at a personal, family, community or workplace level, either as a proposer and developer of such policies or as someone who has to live with the declared policy. Two problems associated with this are, first, there may be some conflict between policy statements for different purposes and, second, that all such policy statements must work within the legal provisions of the jurisdiction, which means they must work with the national statutory provision but also with the national sense about what information policy should be.

A complication arises when the state apparatus is weak and the enforcement of law inconsistent; in these cases lower level entities, families, community or other organizations, and even individuals, will need to formulate information policies that work within the unsupportive environment. In these circumstances there may be an extra need to protect personal data, probably by withholding it, and an extra need to protect intellectual property and to find ways of accessing necessary information held by other state and non-state agencies. Thus information policies will vary from any standard 'western democratic' model, and this variation will take account not only of the different working environment but also of the varying chances of any of the sector mechanisms we discussed in Part 2 being effective.

Obligations

Two final considerations should be noted before we move on to policy formation. First, we need to review the relationship between information policy and truth. It might seem axiomatic that a good information policy would emphasize truth values throughout. Yet it is actually not necessary, in fact almost impossible, to do so. If we require all information that is generated or transferred to have a correspondence to the truth in any empirical sense we are saddling ourselves with a definition of information that is unsustainable. For example, it would exclude all fictional material. Second, it would put on us a requirement to find some way of verifying the truth value of any information to be transferred. Third, it would not take account of variations in scientific knowledge, and we would have an unacceptably authoritarian information regime if, when scientific knowledge evolved, all previous versions of 'true knowledge' were destroyed. We need, as one of the checks on information and knowledge, to be able to trace its development. Information policy becomes a policy about the transfer of what claims to be information, and the policy maker makes no judgements about those claims. It would, however, be quite reasonable to require people who are transferring information to attest to their sincere belief about the truth of the information they are conveying. So, when I make a declaration about my name or address I should tell the truth, and I similarly expect information I access to be true in that way.

People have to have confidence about the information they use, but we cannot test for the truth value of all information. So, I can believe and be willing to pass on the knowledge that J. K. Rowling wrote a book about a boy wizard without needing to have any confidence as to whether there really was a boy wizard. When we deal with governments and the information they release the situation is slightly more complicated. When I ask for all documents used by the Department for Transport that relate to a decision to build a new high-speed rail line close to my house I need to have confidence that the documents released to me constitute all the relevant documents and that those documents correspond exactly to those used by the government officials and are not some anodyne substitutes. I may also want to believe that the information in the documents – say something like studies of traffic flows – is 'true', but I may be seeking the documents because I believe the government has based its case on inaccurate information. In this case it may be that the government maintains that the content is 'true', but I may choose not to believe that, and I would be contesting the truth claims in the documents without rejecting the document itself. As most documents go through various drafts there is almost always some variation in text, so making a statement about what constitutes the manuscript for a famous novel almost always involves some level of variation and maybe variation between manuscript copy and the printed book, or variations between manuscripts.

Our second concern is about the moral force of information policies and their relation to the idea of duty. Rights are often expressed as things we owe to other people, and many information policy provisions have a certain moral force. At times people deliberately seek to break taboos about what may or may not be put in print, either because they believe that their art requires that certain things be said, or because they believe that there should be no limits on what may be said. But broadly we are shocked by some art that does break established taboos, even though we may come quickly to accept the new boundaries of legitimate action. At the start of this book we mentioned the case that newspapers and the reading public, and the same is true for broadcast media, have a sense of where the boundaries lie for discussing national secrets, and that everyone played the game within the rules. This is another instance of there being some moral force governing the disclosure and use of information. In this and many other cases we sense that we have a duty not to cross that boundary. However, in this case the moral injunction is not about the information *per se* but about the national security situation. Should information policies recognize moral imperatives? There is a good case to say that although information policy may rely on the strength of moral arguments in a society to ensure conformity to the policy, and to support enforcement of it, there are few obvious grounds for incorporating any sense of duty or moral force into policy statements. As with the case of national security and secrets, the moral imperatives come from the substantive issue rather than any utterance in itself.

Policy formation
Information policy and theories of information
We can also legitimately ask if, for any comprehensive treatment of information policy, we should consider how information policy relates to theories of information. There is a wide range of theories of information, and most of the discussion about semantic theories of information focuses on issues related to information retrieval and questions closer to cognitive science, and these are of no concern to information policy, nor will they have any impact on policy or policy analysis because they are largely technical discussions. There are other theories of information that can be described as social theories of information. They go under various labels according to how they are generated, but they all claim that information is a social construction. These claims about information do relate to our ideas about information policy, but there is no direct connection linking our notion of information to policy. The most we can say at present is that if – and so far these claims about information are only claims – information is a social construction then we must consider it alongside information policy because, obviously, information policy is a social construction too.

Autonomy in information policy

In chapters 2 and 3 the idea of information policy as autonomous was mentioned. This description was used for situations where information policy instruments, giving effect to policy areas like censorship or data protection, or any other area, were seen as developing independently of particular conditions. So, where, say, censorship, exists to serve a particular social need, if the instrument of censorship continued after the particular social need had passed we could say that it was autonomous. That is to say that it has an existence independent of the particular set of social conditions that bring it into existence, or that it exists independently of any theoretical explanation of society like information society or public sphere theories. An autonomous policy can obviously be connected to the idea of a strong theory of information policy, but it is not coterminous with that idea because even though it has autonomous existence it may still not be sufficient or necessary cause – and therefore be closer to a weak theory of policy – for a social phenomenon like an information society.

Strong and weak theories of information policy

Although there are available theories of information we so far have little that can count as a theory of information policy. In chapters 2 and 3 we discussed the idea of strong and weak theories of information policy, but these were really labels to cover the cases where information policies act as determinants for the existence of either information societies or public spheres. Where information policies come to exist because an information society, or the concept of an information society, brings them into being we can say that we have a weak theory of information policy. Where the existence of an information society is dependent on, and in character is determined by, information policy we have a strong theory of information policy. A point to elaborate here is that we could try to put together empirical evidence to substantiate such a claim, but it is more likely that we could construct some explanation of information societies that embedded information policy in the theoretical construction of how such societies work.

Actually, we can go farther than that, and work to construct the elements of a theory that might explain the development of information policy, but we have to contend with two intervening problems. First, policy for individual sectors, like censorship or intellectual property protection, seem to be largely independent and in no way wholly bound in to any integrated information policy that covered all aspects of information generation and transfer. Second, unless information policy theory is constructed as part of something else we would have to show a level of independence for information policy that hitherto we have not had empirical evidence to support. There is little point in trying to construct a theory of anything unless there is either a phenomenon that needs a theoretical explanation or because a theory will enable us to build further hypotheses and extend our knowledge of the subject. At present neither of those conditions has been met for information policy, with the caveat that, as mentioned above, because there is so little comprehensive integrative work on across-the-board information policies, some theoretical work might assist discussion and indicate avenues for further development for information policy as a whole, rather than for individual sectors. One final point that we should note here is that theory for analysis and research may be different from any theory generated either for campaigners or for people trying to construct actual policy. If we did have a theory of information policy the subject might be better able to make a contribution to the development of information science.

Information policy and information science

Information science has developed largely in technical competencies and in experimental work on information retrieval or empirical studies of various information phenomena. So far work on information policies, although occupying a corner of the field, has made neither a substantial contribution to information science's understanding of itself nor has work on information policy developed theories or empirical problems that could have given it a more central position in information science. According to many commentators information science itself is in want of a central unifying theory or concept of the subject, and is still in part the scene of methodological competition between those who want an empirical laboratory science and those who want a broader and more inclusive perspective, which could include humanistic and social science themes and approaches. Therefore it must seem that the ground is wide open for anything, including a methodologically well equipped study of information policy, to lead information science into its next phase of subject development. However, it is unlikely that information policy studies will be able to do that unless it quickly develops a set of problems that are perceived as central to information science and a theoretical and methodological apparatus to serve study in the area. If information policy were to meet those criteria it is likely that it would be seen as an autonomous set of problems and solutions that were independent of other factors.

Information policy and communications policy

Information policy is, largely, about content, and communications policy is, mostly, about channel management and concentrates on issues of technology. The two overlap in some matters. Mobile phone use and regulation is an example, where regulating the carrier is a communications policy issue, but regulating use is a concern of information policy. Should one of these policies be seen as subordinate or part of the other? Obviously, they relate to each other, so in cases of conflict does either command priority? Communications policy has more immediate day to day interest because users are paying to use the services which have in a short time become essential parts of our lives. There are controversial aspects to the technology, too, which commands attention – the use of mobile phones to detonate bombs, the easy use of the technology by criminals or terrorists or others to plan and execute illegal acts, the as yet unproven radiation risks attached to mobile phone use, the high charges for certain types of use, the problem of illegal and harmful content on the internet, and of course the problem of a clogged web as spam takes over the world.

The internet remains largely unregulated, partly because of different information regimes, and different levels of policing and redress, in different countries. The technology of the internet requires national communications authority agreement in international treaties, but the general aim of improved international communications is a powerful driver that helps secure progress. The content of the internet is largely outside national control, and recent EU decisions have distributed the problem to the parliaments of member states to solve. With both mobile (cellular) phones and the internet we can caricature the situation as one where technology secures improved communication, and is therefore approved as a necessary advance and poses no problem for communications policy, but the content carried may include undesirable material which remains an information policy issue.

Communications policy is rarely in the hands of just one authority – often responsibility is split between telecommunications and broadcasting. Information policy is even more widely separated, with several commissioners or commissions for broadcasting, films, videos and print media, with no standard regulatory model, with current practice ranging from self policing for printed newspapers through the use of regulators and agents, to statutory provision for obscene publications. Communications policy concerns the big money items, but information policy, as a general issue for public discussion, ranges over a wider number of issues, and can also include trade issues in information products and services. The picture is not clear cut, but it is possible to discuss information policy issues as abstract or general questions, as we have done, without having to tie the discussion to communication policy. The two are not coterminous, and although they have many objects in common they tend to look at different aspects of each issue, but as it is the more general topic, we can say that information policy could include communications policy.

Information policy, strategy and information management

At the start of this book we indicated a need to differentiate between policy, strategy and information management. Later on we also indicated that what are simple preferences should not be confused with policy. The example of choosing to give presents of books at Christmas was stated to be a preference and not a policy. Similarly we can safely say that many other practices are more closely connected to information management than information policy. So, the decision to collect all your music on your iPod is partly a preference and possibly a management decision, but it is not a policy matter. Why can we say this? It became apparent in the discussion about overarching theories of society that we employ the term 'information policy' not as a simple label or description but in a complex of ways to describe not only a relationship to the theory of society in question but also the way that society uses instruments to give effect to its ideas about the generation, use and exchange of information. Neither information management nor preferences cover the generation of information: the techniques used to secure certain information policy objectives might come within a general description of information management but those objectives are derived from a higher level process of analysis than information management can provide.

We are left with the need to distinguish information policy and information policy strategies. For convenience we could put the two terms in a hierarchy and say that strategies are used to achieve policy objectives. Are we then saying that the policy objectives arise from the kinds of considerations that arose in Part 1 of this book and that the sectoral mechanisms used in Part 2 are the strategies? This is probably not the case, and we might be happier without drawing that direct relationship. If we use the two terms in a loose sense it would immediately become clear that the terms are not interchangeable: policies are not strategies. However, we can use the two terms as indicated above and use strategies to implement policies. The strategies might become an intermediate step between policies overall, or policy for a particular sector, and the mechanisms and instruments used to give effect to them. So, we could say that there is a policy of rewarding creativity by relying on market mechanisms, and a strategy of using the law to create the environment for that to work.

Outcomes: desires, intentions and objectives

The process of drafting information policies varies according to the working environment. If you are devising a personal information policy, or one for a family, it is most unlikely that you would write it down: it would just be something you worked out mentally and attempted to keep to. In other circumstances a written policy is more useful. For all circumstances we need to distinguish between desires, intentions, objectives and policies. This is a continuation and extension of the last point raised in the previous section.

Policies are usually more than expressions of desires or even of intentions. You may think 'I wish there was less violence on TV', and that is just an expression of a desire, it is not a policy. Similarly, setting the intention – 'I intend to reduce the level of violence on TV' is no more than an indication of an as yet unsettled plan of campaign. However, we must also recognize that policies may be very broad statements that do encompass desires and intentions but go much further and probably are supported by justifications, even though the level of detail may be very general. Policy statements relate the point about which the policy is made to more general conditions that indicate why the policy is needed. So, staying with the intellectual property example, we could have a policy that indicated the decision to reward creativity by relying on market mechanisms that was supported by two distinct lines of argument – first, that there is a need in society to encourage creativity, and second, that alternative measures, like expert assessment, are no more likely to be fair or accurate than market assessments, which require less administration.

Contexts

That argument places an added emphasis on contexts, which we can regard in two ways. First, in the general sense of contexts, we can write in descriptions of contexts, rather as acts of parliament or international treaties have a preamble, which gives the general reasons behind the agreement to act. These descriptions also act as statements of justification. Such a description of context could include very general contexts, not necessarily related at all to the information policy issue that is being addressed. There are obvious circumstances like war or emergencies or technological developments that might make it necessary to introduce new or amending legislation in a wide range of topics. A second way in which we can use context is to embed the context in the policy. This is appropriate when the argument about the policy is closely related to the external context and is in some way dependent on it. An example would be any argument developed about information policy within the public sphere or the information society that tied control of information into the general argument and required that context to be made explicit, as an explanation.

The difference between the two types of context is that in the more general case it is less likely that elements of the context will become integral aspects of the argument for the information policy. In the second case, where it is most likely that the context is itself a theoretical construction, or at least an abstract argument about some new empirical condition – new telecommunication structures, for example, the arguments for the information policy, and any strategies and mechanisms that are entailments of the policy, will be closely related to the claims about the context and one will inform the other to a degree of detail that will not apply in the more general case. A further question we should consider is whether or not such a closely tied-in context, with interlocking arguments, will have an across the board effect on all information policy components. That brings us to the question of integrated information policies.

Integrated information policies

In Chapter 1 we noted that information policy is rarely integrated, and that attempts to integrate it are most likely to appear in non-democratic states. We should note that there is no reason in principle why information policies should not be integrated, even in democratic societies, but we would have to make some provision for important and well regarded aspects of democratic life. There is a pluralism in democratic societies, by which we normally mean that institutions and individuals are not in a hierarchic relationship, with the intentions and actions of all being determined from one central point. Pluralism means that the decision making process depends on agreement between major participants. If we were to impose an integrated set of information policies it is possible that the character of communication and information transfer and use could be set to benefit one particular set of interests and that might endanger the pluralist structure. However, we have no means of predicting that, but we can say that where pluralist structures exist there is a reduced likelihood of integrated information policies being adopted, because each institution and participant would act to secure their own interest and the possibility of reduced capacity to communicate and transfer information would not gain their consent.

Against these observations we could put the conjecture that in some future potential Habermasian public sphere, where there was a secure degree of reciprocity and all participants enjoyed equality and where the test of an acceptable utterance was its rationality, we could see an integrated information policy gaining consent. But, that policy would have to support and maintain – and have as one of its major external objectives – the Habermasian public sphere. What would such an information policy seek to establish and maintain as an internal objective? The recognition of rational thought and its expression, and its rapid transmission to arenas for discussion would obviously be important. We can speculate, but unless we do some analysis, using some derivative of the Cohen model, we are unlikely to be able to determine what intellectual property regime would be preferred but it would certainly be one that facilitated the free flow of ideas. We can also say with some certainty that such a public sphere would rely on some general moral imperatives to act as a restraining influence on utterances, for it would be unthinkable to have a formal restraint on what could be said or seen – there could be little or no censorship. By extension, there would be a maximum amount of freedom of information, because open and informed discussion of the business of government would be an essential part of the public sphere. As the autonomy of individuals would have to be respected, so protecting their ability to participate in the public discussions, data protection would have to be strong. Thus many of the set objectives would be determined by the commitment to maintain the public sphere, and the internal coherence would also be required by the same need. The integration would be secured by the need to ensure that there was no conflict between the various elements of the integrated policy, as any appeal to an external authority to resolve disputes would be an indication of a breakdown in the structure of the policy. At present conflict between policy components is normally resolved through appeal to the legal process.

This conjecture about what might be expected in a Habermasian space also gives us an indication of what might be found in non-democratic states, where information policy will be either capricious and haphazard or constructed intentionally to serve the needs of the ruling elite or the dominant ideology. Thus the strongly characteristic element in integrated information policies is subservience to an external objective, whereas in our pluralist world information policies are normally constructed to meet the needs of a specific information problem, but the interests being served may casually benefit the strongest voice.

Drafting information policy

We have reviewed many factors affecting the conception and implementation of information policy, and we have, at length, worked to develop an analytical device to help us analyse what we want to protect or discard in our information policies. We need more than an adaptation of Cohen's model for securing free speech if we are to develop policy statements successfully. That model, or rather the abstraction that we developed from it, can only indicate the central elements of what we seek to secure; we also need two other instruments. First, a statement, derived from description and analysis, of the information problem that we are seeking a policy for, expressed both in general terms and also in a semi-technical form that allows us to identify the point that information policy can act upon. Second, or rather third as the analytical model is the second operation, we need to draft the instruments that give effect to the intentions. The intentions become apparent from our use of the abstract analytic model that we developed in Part 2. The third element, the instrument or mechanism, is the set of procedures that will give effect to the intentions. The appropriateness and success of this third statement can be measured against the first and second statements. The first statement relates both to our general understanding of the problem – what might go into a preamble – and our expression of intentions, objectives and outcomes. It will set the terms of what is to be discussed. The second statement, generated after working through the analytic model, gives a set of concrete points to achieve, and that will play a part too as a test of the final statement laying out the means. This last point is important, as are mechanisms to monitor performance.

It would be simple and natural to think that the normal instrument or mechanism would be some change in the law, and it is most likely that some legal provision would be necessary, but this would be too simplistic. Law looms large in our consciousness about information policy, and that is a reflection of many influences. The role of the state, both as agent and as the object of campaigns, has meant that law, as the instrument of state power and as the only means of compelling the state, figures prominently. Although this is true, and that legislation is almost inevitably a significant part of information policy, both in determination of what it is and in implementation and enforcement, we should not ignore other important elements in the overall structure of information policy formation and execution.

There are many elements in all societies that play powerful and influential roles in fixing our ideas about what policy should attempt to achieve – in other words, the moral horizons and intentions are determined by institutions like religion, education, the consciousness of the history of the state or nation, as well as by more immediate pressures like economic circumstances or operating requirements. In this broader picture legislation plays a part but that only works because we have, in our history, constructed societies that see law as a benign agent of change and improvement. The role of custom and of long established procedures and processes, which also play a part in setting the fame for policy decisions and execution, need to be enclosed within our picture of what determines information policy. Similarly, at an operational level, the law may set objectives but the actual processes may be agreed and set up without need for legislation, by administrative action under the authority of legislation or treaties, or by simple agreement. What is also clear is that legislation alone is inadequate: some means of implementation and enforcement is essential.

Monitoring and evaluating information policies

There is no standard provision for monitoring or evaluating information policies, although a system to review all policies and legislative provision would be useful. There are many organizations that monitor existing conditions and laws and campaign for improvements for the people or groups they represent. Although they may work, sometimes with others, to effect a general improvement in laws or systems or practices, especially when new technologies need to be incorporated into existing structures, it is not certain that they would work for a general public interest change in law. Sometimes laws in particular sectors incorporate provisions for review, and sometimes the laws are put in place for limited periods of time, requiring new laws or a resolution of the legislature for a continuation. When new laws also involve new institutions or bureaucracies that are set up to make a new system work effectively

– such as with offices for information commissioners or ombudsmen – governments have an effective control over the operation of the law through their control of funding. Underfunding offices so they cannot get through all the business that has built up is an effective, much disliked, but well known way of defeating the intentions of legislators. There are broader reasons for reviewing the effect of information policy overall, as well as that for separate sectors, but the overall picture mostly suffers from lack of attention.

Do we really need information policies?

Our daily experience of information policy as reported in the media is not of a coherent system but of actions within well known problem areas such as censorship and intellectual property regulation, and more recently of the other two topics we have discussed in Part 2 and with some that we have not, like communications or broadcasting regulation. All these topics seem to have separate lives of their own, and the specific character of problems in these areas, and the characteristic search for legal solutions, dominate discussion and thinking. There is rarely any reference, except as a casual acknowledgement of them as a label for the era we are in, of any higher level concept like the information society or the public sphere. Human rights are occasionally referred to, but not in any sense of there being a recognizable group of information rights or any recognition of them as a distinct way to regulate information generation, use and exchange.

The rush of life makes this understandable, but in our haste we lose sight of the importance of information policy, an importance implicitly recognised by Habermas in his conceptualization of the public sphere. The regulation of information, and indeed the need not to regulate much of it, is seen as one part of the complex of mechanisms that sustain effective social and political life, especially in democracies; we should keep to the fore the realization that the way information is regulated is constitutive of social and political life, making possible the form and character of what we can say and read, and thus framing what kind of society we can have, and what we allow in democratic deliberations. Information policy is crucial and critical to sustain the most flexible, most accountable, and most resilient form of political life human society has ever invented, and we should give all our information policies, the reasons for having them, and the means of achieving them, our very best attention.

References and reading list

Bell, D. (1973) *The Coming of Post-Industrial Society*, Penguin.

Benhabib, S. (1992) Models of Public Space: Hannah Arendt, the liberal tradition, and Jurgen Habermas. In Benhabib, S., *Situating the Self: gender, community and postmodernism in contemporary ethics*, Polity Press, 89–120.

Branscomb, A. W. (1985) Property Rights in Information. In Guile, B. (ed.), *Information Technologies and Social Transformation*, National Academy Press, 81–120.

Branscomb, A. W. (1988) Who Owns Creativity?: property rights in the information age, *Technology Review* (May/June), 39–44.

Calhoun, C. (ed.) (1992) *Habermas and the Public Sphere*, MIT Press.

Clark, C. (1940) *The Conditions of Economic Progress*, Macmillan.

Cohen, J. (1993) Freedom of Expression, *Philosophy and Public Affairs*, **22** (3), 207–63.

Habermas, J. (1989) *The Structural Transformation of the Public Sphere: an enquiry into a category of bourgeois society*, Polity Press.

Habermas, J. (1993) Further Reflections on the Public Sphere. In Calhoun, C. C. (ed.), *Habermas and the Public Sphere*, MIT Press, 421–61.

Hettinger, E. C. (1989) Justifying Intellectual Property, *Philosophy and Public Affairs*, **18** (Winter), 31–52.

Koselleck, R. (1988 [1959]) *Critique and Crises: enlightenment and the pathogenesis of modern society*, MIT Press.

Machlup, F. (1962) *The Production and Distribution of Knowledge in the United States*, Princeton University Press.

Oyen, E. (1982) Confidentiality, Theory and Practice, *Current Sociology*, **30** (2), 1–37.

Privacy Protection Study Commission (1977) *Personal Privacy in an Information Society: report of the Privacy Protection Study Commission*, USGPO.

Stehr, N. (1995) *Knowledge Societies*, Sage.

Touraine, A. (1971) *The Post-Industrial Society: tomorrow's social history: classes, conflicts and culture in the programmed society*, Random House.

Universal Declaration of Human Rights (1948) www.un.org/en/documents/udhr/.

Villa, D. R. (1992) Postmodernism and the Public Sphere, *American Political Science Review*, **86** (3), 712–21.

Waldron, J. (1987) *'Nonsense Upon Stilts': Bentham, Burke and Marx on the Rights of Man*, Methuen.

Index